Somehow

Somehow

THOUGHTS ON LOVE

Anne Lamott

RIVERHEAD BOOKS

NEW YORK

2024

RIVERHEAD BOOKS
An imprint of Penguin Random House LLC
penguinrandomhouse.com

Copyright © 2024 by Anne Lamott
Penguin Random House supports copyright. Copyright fuels creativity,
encourages diverse voices, promotes free speech, and creates a vibrant culture.
Thank you for buying an authorized edition of this book and for complying
with copyright laws by not reproducing, scanning, or distributing any part of
it in any form without permission. You are supporting writers and allowing
Penguin Random House to continue to publish books for every reader.

Riverhead and the R colophon are registered trademarks
of Penguin Random House LLC.

Coleman Barks's translation of the Rumi poem "The Guest House" originally
published in *The Essential Rumi*, copyright 2004 by Coleman Barks.
HarperCollins Publishers, New York, NY, USA.

LIBRARY OF CONGRESS CATALOGING-IN-PUBLICATION DATA
Names: Lamott, Anne, author.
Title: Somehow : thoughts on love / Anne Lamott.
Description: New York : Riverhead Books, 2024.
Identifiers: LCCN 2023033482 (print) | LCCN 2023033483 (ebook) |
ISBN 9780593714416 (hardcover) | ISBN 9780593714423 (ebook)
Subjects: LCSH: Love. | Lamott, Anne. | Novelists, American—
20th century—Biography. | LCGFT: Essays.
Classification: LCC PS3562.A4645 S66 2024 (print) |
LCC PS3562.A4645 (ebook) | DDC 814/.54—dc23/eng/20230809
LC record available at https://lccn.loc.gov/2023033482
LC ebook record available at https://lccn.loc.gov/2023033483

Printed in the United States of America
1st Printing

Book design by Amanda Dewey

For Jax

CONTENTS

The Guest House

This being human is a guest house.
Every morning a new arrival.
A joy, a depression, a meanness,
some momentary awareness comes
as an unexpected visitor.
Welcome and entertain them all!
Even if they are a crowd of sorrows,
who violently sweep your house
empty of its furniture,
still, treat each guest honorably.
He may be clearing you out
for some new delight.
The dark thought, the shame, the malice,
meet them at the door laughing,
and invite them in.
Be grateful for whoever comes,
because each has been sent
as a guide from beyond.

~ RUMI, translated by Coleman Barks

Somehow

Overture

My husband said something a few years ago that I often quote: Eighty percent of everything that is true and beautiful can be experienced on any ten-minute walk. Even in the darkest and most devastating times, love is nearby if you know what to look for. It does not always appear at first to be lovely but instead may take the form of a hot mess or a snoring old dog or someone you have sworn to never, ever forgive (for a possibly very good reason, if you ask me). But mixed in will also be familiar signs of love: wings, good-hearted people, cats (when they are in the right mood), a spray of wildflowers, a cup of tea.

What are we even talking about when we talk about love? What is it?

I asked a six-year-old friend of mine.

"Oh, it's just this *stuff*," he said, rolling his eyes.

I think that's right.

Love is caring, affection, and friendliness, of course, compassion and a generous heart. It is also some kind of energy or vibration, because everything is—the same stuff moving at different speeds, from glaciers to six-year-old boys.

I wish the movement of love in our lives more closely resembled the grace of a ballerina, but no, love mainly tromps and plops, falls over and tiptoes through our lives.

Love looks like us, and that can be a little daunting. Love is why we are here at all, on the couch and in the world with a heart for the common good, why we have hope, and a lifeline when we don't.

There is sweet family love, entangled by history, need, frustration, and annoyance. There is community love, a love of music, Zorba's reckless love of life. It can be vital or serene. There's the ecstatic love—for the natural world, or in bed—there's the love of justice or the radical transforming love of what we might call Goodness, Gus (the Great Universal Spirit), or God.

Love is often hard, ignored, or hilarious (eventually). Love looks like you—to me and a few others. And this is the hardest thing to believe.

One thing is certain: Love is our only hope. Love springs from new life, love springs from death. Love acts like Gandhi and our pets and Jesus and Mr. Bean and Mr. Rogers and Bette Midler. Love just won't be pinned down. Love is Florence Nightingale and Coyote Trickster, who messes with us by way of his teachings about how we might possibly, grudgingly, awaken to the glory of life. Love is the warmth we feel in the presence of a favorite aunt, the kindness of a waitress, and the warmth of the hand that pulls us back to our feet when the loss of love has all but destroyed us. It is this stuff, which any kid and most poets will tell you we experience in our hearts.

Nonsense, you may say: love arises and is regulated in a part of the brain called the amygdala. How right you are, once again! And how happy that must make you, as it often does me, and why I so need the intervention of love. Do I want to be right or to have a loving heart? And will this be on the test? My brain also controls my breathing, but man, do I love my lungs.

On a ten-minute walk anywhere—from outside my gate with its broken latch to the loudest block in Brooklyn to Garbage City in Cairo—love abounds and abides, flirts and weeps with us. It is there for the asking, which is the easy part. Our lives' toughest work is in the receiving. Love presents most obviously in babies and kids being cuddled, yet also as patience with annoying humans we live or work with or are. We feel love upon seeing our favorite neighbors and first responders, we see it in fundraising efforts, peace marches, kindergarten classrooms, gardens. When flowers don't stir feelings of love in me, something is gumming up the works.

In a ten-minute walk from home the other day, I passed a house with a new baby, another with a recent death, then two houses down a loud argument between a usually devoted couple; an English garden, an abandoned shack behind woodpiles on a desolate lot, boxes of bees buzzing honey into existence, and terrified parents chasing after little kids careening away on their first two-wheelers.

I have lived in this neighborhood for nearly two decades, and I know every house on the block. I have nursed a woman and her small children through her way-too-early death and been there for the family across the street when their twenty-one-year-old child jumped off the Golden Gate Bridge. On our first date, I brought my future husband home to the house where, seven years earlier, my nineteen-year-old son had brought home his first child. We helped raise Sam's boy in the tiny grassy park right across the street. (Nana and Neal are tree-huggers.) I stood in the same street with my addict son in 2011 with a sharpened pencil held near his throat and told him he could not come back until he stopped using, and then welcomed him back a month later with ten days clean and sober, twelve years ago tomorrow. We in the 'hood isolated during COVID and walked six feet away from one another as lovingly as we could, waving. Waving can be love, as well as stop-and-chats and shouted compliments on their camellia bush. We did what we could to help one another and the very poor a few miles away. Our ninety-year-old neighbor Jesse passes by on his walks every day. Way too many arrogant and ecstatic bicyclists race too fast past him and me on their way to the water district ponds, where flotillas of ducks paddle by and egrets stand looking like Bernie Sanders with their unruly haircuts and posture. Our dogs had their last meals of hot dogs and ice cream here in the corner park on their way to whatever awaits us all, breaking our hearts forever until we brought our next dogs here to meet the team. We stood outside on days before elections and promised each other that the unthinkable was not going to happen, and then when it did, we met here again the next day, clutch-ing our heads.

A few minutes' walk from my front door, un-housed people come to sit on a memorial bench in the shade kitty-corner from the park, one of whom is my woolly friend Ben. The neighbors pile giveaways on the bench—clothes, egg poachers, and baby gear—infuriating some neighbors, who vent on Nextdoor about the unsightly mess, but a bless-ing to others—i.e., to me. This bench itself was carved by a townsperson long ago—live-edge and beautifully rustic. It holds us all: me, Ben, Jesse.

When we are paying attention, we see how much holds us invisibly. Love is a bench.

There are two benches in the little park and eight redwoods. Tightrope walkers set up their wire above the grass and practice for hours. Older peo-ple faithfully do tai chi early in the day. Dog people sit together and catch up while their dogs run and play. One small dog ran into the street recently and got hit, but she lives on joyfully with three legs. After dark in the summer, teenagers get drunk and stoned here and then drive away, leaving their litter behind. My grandson has just turned fourteen and because I love him more than anything, my heart is often in my throat. Love can be very scary. In fact, love is actually scary about half the time.

Menace abounds. It was 107 degrees out today. We smell the smoke from distant fires. Men steal our catalytic converters while we sleep. Men who were not shown love do terrible things in the world, and love shows up as volunteers, nurses, best friends. Love shows up with food and antibiotics. Love shows up with tea.

Years ago my friend Caroline found a small frog in a shower that was being remodeled, so she picked it up and carried it in her cupped hands to the wet grass outside. The frog was leaping in terror against her hands as she carried it, and probably did not understand the quiet comforting words she spoke to it along the way. I think this is one of the best examples of how love operates when we are most afraid and doomed, carrying us to a safer place while we pound against its cupped hands.

I teach my Sunday school kids that love is God and God is love. The God of my understanding is baffled by what *isn't* love. It's unfathomable to God to imagine not loving. The Dominican friar Timothy Radcliffe wrote that God can never tell you not to love someone. God can only tell you to do a better job loving someone. (God is somewhat better at this than I.)

Love is interconnectedness. We grew up learning that tree roots are always competing for space and nutrients, but since then we've learned that beneath the ground is a lacy network of communication and help. Redwood roots spread in shallow, interlaced webs barely under the surface, keeping any single tree straight against the wind. If one tree gets sick or harmed, other trees send it their nutrients and supplies. Love is a root system. (Trees are better at this than I am.) But I see all around me that we evolve, slowly, over time, often in community. The Jesuit Teilhard de Chardin believed that against all evidence, we are all evolving toward Christ consciousness, but maybe if he had lived in the modern scientific age he might have tied in tree consciousness, toward oneness and sharing. And maybe they are the same thing.

Love is evolutionary, survival of the species. Not-love is killing us.

Maybe love is our very atmosphere, the one energy that Einstein describes as being that which is the only thing there is. This would mean that love is like Wi-Fi, always and already here (if a bit wobbly sometimes), sight unseen, until we look around and begin to notice and use love's atoms and agents, the one-dimensional vibrating strings with which all life is composed. Maybe love is a radio station that we can tune to, when we can turn away from

the crack cocaine of news and the internet to Bach
and sambas and "Taps," to melodious sonnets and
the Beatles.

One walks along mulling over old hurts and
new ways to save and rescue family members—
good luck with that—and ingenious schemes for
alleviating the national political madness, world
starvation, disease, tribal wars. Love often looks
like grief. Love seems to be good friends with death,
although I would prefer it was better friends with
comfort and mirth. Love is compassion, which Neal
defines as the love that arises in the presence of
suffering. Are love and compassion up to the stark
realities we face at the dinner table, and down the
street, and at the melting ice caps, or within Ira-
nian nuclear plants and our own Congress?

Maybe; I think so. Somehow.

Love's loss is the source of most suffering, and
then love transforms the suffering into depth, compassion, and the great painful gift of humility. I
never love this. One day at a time, and sometimes
one hour at a time, love will be enough to see us
through, get us back on our feet and dust us off.
Love gives us a shot at becoming the person we
were born to be, not the charming actor or bodyguard we became, not us on our tightropes holding

our breath as we strive for greatness (or at any rate not falling on our butts). When all is said and done, and against all odds, love is sufficient unto the day.

Could I be wrong? Obviously. But I don't think I am. Love is what our soul is made of, and for. Love is a piece of toast and a diamond. It is a sturdy and imperfect shelter, all around and deep inside, a lantern with warm bracing light, a magician. When life has lost its promise, or disappointed us one too many times, when it is hard to trust again or feel alive and curious again, love beckons us over and asks, "Got a minute?"

What is there to lose? A lot—familiarity, complacency, the illusion of control. And what is there to gain? A chance to loosen up and lighten up and sometimes even live it up, a chance to feel the warmth of this gentle, wild, messy, holy world. So I'll ask you, too: Got a minute?

ONE

Swag

Hell in a handbasket was the good old days, back in another century when smog and Nixon were the emergencies. What can I leave my son and grandson by way of general instructions for when I am gone? What has consistently worked to lift us and light the way during the inevitable times of deep darkness?

There is a story I live by, which I have been telling my Sunday school kids for thirty years now, and which they never tire of, or least have the good sense to still pretend to enjoy if they have any hope of getting snacks. A young girl is having a hard time falling asleep one night and calls out for her mother. Her mother comes in and gently tucks her in again and assures her that Jesus is there in the room with her, so she needn't be afraid. This goes on and on, each time the increasingly annoyed mother saying basically the same thing until finally, in the dark, the little girl says plaintively, "I need someone with skin on."

This is the main instruction that I would leave my family in my swag bag of spiritual truth: be goodness with skin on. Most days this will be enough. Also, be sure to plant bulbs in the winter, help the poor, and light candles in the dark to see where you are, where you've been, what remains, and how much still works just fine. That last one will amaze you.

We are called to be the love that wears socks and shoes, like God's Love We Deliver, the secular group based in New York City whose volunteers bring food to the sick and dying. I have "GLWD" inscribed on the ring I wear on my right hand so I can remember that if you want to have loving feelings, do loving things. You take a bag of canned food and Oreos to the nearest food bank. You call your cranky uncle to say hello and stay on the phone even after he goes into full weirdness. You foster old pets or donate to people who do. There are nearly infinite ways to be love in communal expression. Our church came up with another good one.

We've had a gorgeous, exuberant new preacher for the last two years named Floyd Thompkins, who is huge in heart and soul. He and the deacons at our tiny church came up with the idea of putting together bags of supplies for the unsheltered in our county, with necessities like shampoo, socks, and dental floss. They did not ask where people without shelter would find water for showers, or the sudden desire to floss. "Figure it out" is not a good slogan. (This would also be a line in my metaphoric swag bag.) They would just give them out freely, like at the Academy Awards.

One Sunday we arrived at church to find not only our oldest elder, Lauretta, taking our temperatures at the door, but also a pile of lavender bags, big ordinary plastic bags, with no branding anywhere. Lavender is a color of royalty, of calming and fairies—ask any little girl. And each bag was filled with items the deacons believed would enhance a person's life.

My lifelong cross to bear has been secret derisive judgment, a pinball machine of sizing up everything and everyone. I am working on it, but the healing is going slightly more slowly than one would hope. So I swallowed my sense that this was ridiculous, took three bags on my way out after service, and threw them on the floor of the back seat of my car.

When I got home, I lifted one bag and noticed that the light shone through it. Peering in, I saw there was actually some thoughtful stuff in there, including a porkpie hat. Some days that might be the only shelter a homeless person had, a kind of roof. It was a very ordinary hat, with holes in its brim so you wouldn't get too sweaty. It was foldable and the label said it was broad-spectrum. I liked that. If we broaden our spectrum, we would see everyone as family, even the craziest "Christian" Congresspeople (theoretically), and obviously refugees and the homeless. These are people and we are all human, made of Big Bang stardust. That's the broad spectrum that we need.

Also, I noted, the hat was water-resistant, a good thing because who knows what might come out of the sky and land on our heads? The bag also had in it two pairs of black socks and some personal hygiene products.

I left the bags on the car floor and did not think about them for a few days, until I saw a scruffy man on a bench on my way home. I pulled over. It was Jesus in His distressing guise as a man in a tattered down jacket in 90-degree weather, smoking.

I got out of my car with my purple bag of love and a bottle of water. I could smell him from ten feet away. I've read that Indigenous people sometimes let layers of oil build up on them from the environment and a little sacred dirt as a form of protection. But, dude, I wanted to say, come on! We are in a busy little hippie bourgeois town.

Luckily for him, I had body wash.

"Hi, I'm Annie!" I said to him. He chewed on his chapped lip as he looked at me. I smiled gently. "I have something for you, because I know that it must be hard to always have things on hand when you need them. Can I sit down?"

He looked anxious, which is appropriate if a nice Christian lady approaches you clutching a big lavender bag. But he moved to the far end of the bench to make room and I sat at the other end. I put the bag between us. He peered over and down, as if off the side of a cliff.

"It's a bag of stuff I put together that everybody needs every day." No judgment here; everyday things for everyday people.

I took out the first item, the toothpaste. The man looked at me askance, like I was offering him an enema bag.

"No, thanks," he said and stubbed out his cigarette on the bench.

I had a tiny position on this, on creating wood burns on handcrafted live-edge benches, when he could have just as easily stubbed it out on the ground. But I kept my Church Lady mouth shut.

Instead I reached inside for the toothbrush and floss. I began babbling out of sheer anxiety. I sounded insane. "Teeth are an incredible problem, aren't they?" I asked. "Cavities, gum disease. And I have to wear this stupid Invisalign retainer on my bottom teeth to correct some teeth that shifted. It hurts, and I have to sit in the orthodontist's waiting room with eleven-year-olds. Hah hah."

He gave me the side-eye but didn't get up, as I might have at this point. And I had many more thoughts: Colgate is a good brand, with a fresh minty taste. And this tube had what it said were Smack Plaque properties. I say smack that damn plaque!

"No, thank you," he said, and lit another cigarette.

I sat quietly beside him, secretly huffing the secondhand smoke, keeping my horrible judgy thoughts to myself. Can't we all agree that flossing says your mouth is worth it? And I personally enjoy it because it's kind of contemplative, twanging that string up and down, a cat's cradle of oral activity.

Somehow

We sat in silence in the sun. Then he lunged for the whole bag, put it in his lap, and started pawing through it. Now I was getting somewhere. He took both pairs of socks and handed the bag back to me.

"That's all I need," he mumbled, and got up to leave.

Wait, what? Did he think I was a 7-Eleven? I wanted to say, "You can't just take that. You have to take the whole bag! There's a system." Instead I said, "So glad you like them." And I was. Really.

I bought some socks to make the bag complete for my next client, but I didn't see any other street people for a while. I really hoped to see my gentle homeless friend Ben, whom I've known for years, but weeks passed and I didn't. I asked around. Everyone knows and loves him—well, except for the parents of the teenagers with whom he plays guitar and smokes dope. He's probably in his late fifties but could be an old forty because that is what street life does to you. I always ask if he's eaten that day and then give him a ten or whatever I have on me. Had he moved away, or even died?

Street people die. One of my Sunday school kids, Michael, became homeless after he graduated from high school; he went to live in a community under a bridge near the harbor two towns over. Some of us from church stayed in touch and tried to save him, but he didn't want to be saved. Then, early one morning, he got shot. The last time we talked, he called with great joy in his voice. "Annie," he said. "I have the best news! My dog had six puppies!" I had an opinion on this, only partly because he had a pit bull, but I simply cooed and told him I loved him. Not long after our call, he was shot and killed.

A few weeks after seeing the homeless man on the bench, I was driving to pick up a friend from church for a funeral of one of our parish saints. In the car I took out my mortifying retainer to eat a snack, and as I put it on the passenger seat, I started admonishing myself—don't put it there! It's almost invisible. You'll lose it. Put it in your purse. But I was running late. I stopped at Safeway to get some water, and when I got out of the car, I saw a mother and child panhandling at the curb. If not homeless, they were clearly destitute. She was holding a sign that said, "Can you help PLEAS!" She was sad and beautiful, with long dark hair and a gold front tooth. The boy was quite handsome and chubby. I fished out a ten-dollar bill from my purse and a purple bag of love from the floor of the back seat. I gave her the bill and then held out the bag. "Here are some really nice things you might like." I held the shampoo (Clairol, another excellent product) and the body wash. I thought, but did not say, that if you could get to a shower, you could really make hay with this, and if not, maybe you could wipe yourself down, like a horse. I pointed out that the body wash was ultra-replenishing, dye-free, paraben-free, and safety-sealed. You could wash in a bathroom sink at Safeway or our local health food store, where most of our town's homeless wash. The woman and I blessed each other several times. I went inside.

When I came out, the purple bag was in the dirt at the curb, and someone had added a bag of cookies. We smiled and blessed each other some more. The boy played on his phone.

I got to where my friend was waiting, threw my purse and napkins in the back seat, and then realized the retainer was gone. My friend and I tore apart the car, checking everywhere: behind and beside the seats, moving them back and forth, beneath the purple bags and my tennis gear. The retainer would cost three hundred dollars to replace. It had to be here somewhere but I'd have to find it later.

Our memorial services are beautiful, soulful, and longggggg, as they tend to be in Black churches. Whole seasons pass. So hours later, my friend and I scoured the car one more time for my retainer. No luck. I dropped her off and raced home to grab a meal so that Neal and I could head to the city for a wedding rehearsal; I was to be the officiant the next day.

I made Neal check the car with me. It was absolutely not there.

Driving to San Francisco, I told Neal we should stop by Safeway and see if the woman and boy were still there, even though there was probably a one percent chance my retainer had landed in the bag. They were still there, with a pile of donated food alongside my bag. I explained that I'd lost a clear plastic retainer and fished through the bag. There it was at the bottom. I burst out laughing. Then I explained to them how grateful I was because the retainer was so expensive to replace and I had given up all hope.

The boy asked, "How much does it cost?"

Uh-oh. I smiled. "One hundred dollars," I lied, wide-eyed, like "Yikes." He thought this over, then rubbed his thumb across his fingertips, the universal sign of give me some money. I laughed and gave his mom a twenty-dollar bill. All that mutual blessing earlier had borne fruit for each of us.

Life delivers the unbelievable so often that you might as well believe.

A month passed. There is a woman in town

with gray dreadlocks all the way down her back, who often gathers them on top of her head and covers them with what looks like a toaster cozy. We often say hi and admire each other's hair. She wears skirts even in winter and her legs are red and covered with welts and sores, but she is sturdy and has warm sweaters and decent teeth. She definitely makes an effort to present as a person of dignity. So one day I pulled over and brought her a bottle of water and a purple bag.

I explained that it was from my church and contained things she might find useful. Here were the antibacterial hand wipes, for instance. Everywhere you turn in this world, there's funk. So someone might use it in a place where there is no toilet paper, like in the bushes behind the post office, which might earn them an outraged write-up in Nextdoor. Not knowing quite what else to say, I pointed out that they were fragrance-free.

"Thanks," she said. We sat down on a bench. I started oversharing again, about not liking products with fragrance. Fragrances are so personal and can be intrusive—people sit in our movie theater reeking of patchouli oil or eat takeout curries. I asked how she felt about this issue. She looked off into space and licked her chapped lips. How had the church neglected to include lip balm?

Her scent was strong and somewhat pleasant, like a girl moose. I handed her the DawnMist body lotion. "This is an excellent lotion," I said rather aggressively, like someone from *Glengarry Glen Ross*. She took it and put it in her lap, and then she patted me on the arm: nice kitty. I felt so warmly toward her that I had to look down. The dawn mist is cold but it means you have gotten through the night. The promise has been fulfilled: the sun has risen. We shared this sweet moment in silence.

She liked the hat but clearly it would be too small for her, with her thick, heavy dreads. She unfolded it. "I could give it to Mick," she said. She folded it back up. "It's very crunchy," she noted. I wondered if that would be a deal-breaker for Mick.

I reached in and took out the Speed Stick de-odorant. I once used it myself. "'All-day fresh and aluminum-free,'" I read in a jocular tone, adding, "Aluminum-free is good, because otherwise you might get Alzheimer's."

What was she supposed to say, "Good to know"?

She looked off into space again. I wanted her to urge Mick to use it: sweat is where your weaknesses show; it's how animals know that you're afraid. So you want to present a really good-smelling front to the dangerous world out there and that's what Speed Stick does for you.

"I have to go," she said.

She started to wipe her nose on her sweater as she rose, so I handed her the packet of pocket tissues. She wiped her nose on the back of her free hand. I gave her the bag and she held it like a brace of pheasants, thanked me again, and headed down the street. The backs of her legs were quite scratched. I should have thought to bring Aquaphor ointment. It's very healing.

These bags were not your ordinary handout. The people at my church in their incredible thoughtfulness had considered how a person might feel cared for. What would help them have a shot at balance? What might help a person who's up against impossible odds?

It's all grassroots, the actions to help another person, one's self, Earth, just small, kind actions. (This statement also belongs in the swag bag.) We are the ones we've been waiting for. No one is going to come save us from our deepest fears. This is so incredibly disappointing.

There's another story I've been telling my kids for thirty years, similar in theme, another scared kid in a dark situation—which is so often me. This one's mother asks him one night to go to the back porch and fetch her the broom. The little boy is too afraid. He cries and begs her not to make him go, but she says there's nothing scary out there, and Jesus is there to help him. So finally the terrified boy goes to the back porch, opens the door a crack, and says, "Jesus, if you're really there, could you hand me the broom?"

It has to be us, getting people brooms and cool drinks of water.

I grieve and feel panicky sometimes about my grandchild's future in the face of climate catastrophe. At the same time, deep in my heart, I do believe. There is a common saying in popular South American songs: "You can cut all the flowers, but you cannot keep spring from coming." Every day people in government try to cut down all the flowers, but spring always comes. So we get people water. There are many kinds. Looking strangers in the eye is water.

Finally, after weeks of worry, I saw Ben again. I got out of my car without a purple bag and told him how happy I was to see him. His eyes were beautiful gray, his nose purple with veins, and the small islands of skin above his beard were sunburned. I told him I had something for him in the car. And he said, "You are so kind to me, Annie. Kindness is how I feel the movement of God."

I thought, "Can I have that line?" Instead, I said he looked well.

I asked if he had shelter from the heat, and he said he and a friend had rigged up a tent under a canopy, like one you'd set up for an outdoor market stand. I asked if it was cozy and he said, slowly, "Oh, it is just fine, Annie." What a radical concept. No plans to upgrade, remodel, move on?

"But what about when the rains come, Ben?"

"My friend and I get everything tightened down in the winter. We've always stayed pretty dry until it warms up again."

"Stay right here," I said. I returned holding the purple bag and a bottle of water and said, "These are some things we put together that might be nice to have in your tent." I offered him the porkpie hat. He put it on and modeled it for me shyly. I nodded yes, very nice, very David Niven. I gave him the two pairs of socks, one for his friend. I put the socks back in the bag and handed him the big bottle of DawnMist body lotion. He studied the ingredients for quite a while. The label declared that the lotion had a fresh bioscent and was pH-balanced, neither acidic nor alkaline. No harm in that, right? We all want that balance, so you don't tip over into exhaustion, into enormous fear and grief, into the ravages of time. The mist is life's way of saying, *We're going to soften the scrim for you now, cut you a break.* You don't always have to see what's in front of you with klieg lights on, because it can be harsh and defeating. Life will make space for all manner of things, but we can get around to those in the fullness of time. For now, some dawn mist. The rains and cold wind will come, the spring will spring like a clown bouquet, the heat rises, the night falls, the sun rises, and we too fall, and rise.

TWO

Shelter

Pink-sherbet camellias blossomed on an otherwise drab, bleak midwinter morning not so long ago. Soon there would be a circus of frivolity, but just now there were twenty or so partially opened flowers. Hundreds of buds hinted at what was in store, each one as tightly packed as a dark green marble. You would have no idea what waited inside. The bush is only a few feet away from our huge living room window, so every year we watch the grand opening from front-row seats as the bush shows its exuberant hand. They were the first camellias of the year, blooming on the same day as my insides felt about to wither and fade.

It all started when I was sitting on the couch with Tim, an old friend from my early days of sobriety. He and his wife, Cory, and I all got sober in 1986; they are ten years younger than I. Over the years I have been there for them when the walls of their psychic shelters were breached: a cancer diagnosis years ago, an affair, a near divorce, infertility. I've often been a kind of spiritual ATM for Tim when he has felt stuck and rattled by the powerlessness du jour. I listen and dispense pretty much the same advice every time: breathe, pray, seek wise counsel, be friendly with yourself, and so on. I bore myself blue sometimes, but that's all I know. He had recently asked me for more intensive mentoring as he sought to find freedom from what he called the bondage of self. He was about to turn fifty-five and craved a reset, freedom from the same ten worries and concerns, freedom from the same ten things he was mad about, freedom from the obsession with the bathroom scale. Freedom from the perfectionism, the disappointment in himself, the dissatisfaction that has run like an underground river through him for a lifetime. Freedom from dragging this all along with him everywhere like a dinosaur's tail. He longed to feel more peaceful, more present and alive.

I was glad to step in, even though like other

nervous cases I do not naturally hearken to the prospect of freedom. I hearken to control and containment. A dark study carrel in the back of the school library would be heaven for me. Life on the couch reading has it all over mountain trails where you could sprain your ankle or be killed by a snake.

I have had more years than Tim of times when walls have come tumbling down, times of hardship that I have later been forced to admit I am grateful for. I know that something shelters me; something somehow both firm and soft holds me up. I have helped Tim be braver a few times. Without seeking outside help, he and his wife stay in one tight, safe, constricted bud. I've reminded him many times over the years that although we were both raised by intellectuals, "Figure it out" turns out not to be a good life slogan. Put down the slide rule, the abacus, the ledger. I've helped him find his deeper inside person: the louder one tells us we are walking bundles of neuroses and issues, but who is the self that notices this? The loud brain is great in some ways—it can do simple math and crossword puzzles, keep us safe in traffic, offer wild entertainment, provide rules of modesty and decorum, distraction, reasons to laugh, and interesting ways to be amused by the world while we're here. But boy, is it an annoying employer.

People love to say enthusiastically that we are here to learn to love reality, to love what is, and my first reaction is that this sounds very angry. Reality includes family hardship, climate change, assault weapons, friends who have died too young, the unfortunate upper arms, and the current Congress. Krishnamurti, when asked how he found peace, said, "I don't mind what happens."

I mind it all.

Reality is so jangly. It's nice and quiet if you stay in bed, or pleasantly distracted with the TV and your personal telecommunications empire. And yet: something in us longs for liberation, for immediacy, and presence. By a certain age, you've figured out you can't go track it down at Machu Picchu, or the Bodhi tree where the Buddha first stops fixating on stupid shit and remembers to breathe. It's not there. It's not at the River Jordan. It's on the couch, where Tim sat beside me with a cup of tea.

I had asked him to prepare a list of the people he was angry at, jealous of, bitter toward, or had hurt feelings or contempt for, and he read it to me. There was a lot of envy, typically of men who still had hair or better jobs or family money. He went on for quite a while. I looked around at the funny little altars nearby that Neal and I create without even thinking about it. Feathers to remind us of flight, weightlessness, grace. Heart-shaped rocks we've found on walks, and glass from the beach that has been tossed and churned, brought to smooth beauty by turbulence.

I listened to Tim share from his most open and vulnerable place, which is paradoxically where we are already most protected, because it's real. Getting old has made me a better listener even as my hearing goes. I leaned in. He spoke of struggling to forgive his wife's really (objectively) awful sister, his boss, a co-worker, a sibling who was still drinking. We finally got to the last person on his list, his close friend Emma.

I do not understand the concept of Emma, whom I know from the community. While she seems perfect on the outside in appearance and charm, I find her a little scary, one of those ebullient people who you secretly think might be packing a .38 Special. She reminds me of what my friend Duncan Trussell says, that when you first meet him, you are actually meeting his bodyguard. Over the years she has hurt Tim's feelings a number of times, with what she imagines is helpful advice on how to be more successful than he has managed to be so far and how to lose a few pounds. She is a sexy librarian type, with her hair often pulled up in a languid bun, oversized glasses, thousand-dollar purses, and perfect breasts, proud and immobile as the lions outside the New York Public Library. I am a little jealous of them. Tim adores her. Most men do. It's a funny thing.

Tim's sturdy wife, Cory, has never seemed jealous, as Tim is not Emma's type, which is handsome and standoffish. Tim is a dog. Emma likes cats.

He told me about Emma's latest weird suggestion, which brilliantly combined advice on his marriage, job, and hair loss. He shared how it made him feel—small, angry—and how tightly he was holding on to it. I nodded from time to time, and idly thought up ways he could get revenge. (This is the Christian way.) He was obsessed—and obsessed with how obsessed he was.

I told him what my mentor of thirty years, Horrible Bonnie, used to tell me when I was tweaking. She described how when a wildebeest has been chased by but finally outrun a lion, it stops and trembles for a while, shaking off the fear hormones until it can shake its way back to its essential wildebeest self.

Tim gripped his head in his hands. "Why do I keep setting myself up for her to put me down and make me feel small?" he asked.

That was a no-brainer. She helped him feel at

home; his dad had been a judge and his mother a first-grade teacher, so feeling condemned and babied was home.

Then something in my pea brain short-circuited. Without thinking, I went after Emma: specifically, how secretly jealous I thought she was of his long and happy marriage. If you asked me, which he hadn't, there was pent-up rage beneath the charming facade. I even went after her fancy new snakeskin purse. We both laughed. It doesn't take Anna Freud to figure out that wearing things made out of dead snake might hint at larger issues.

Tim took this all in, with surprise and curiosity at my cheerful malice. But I didn't stop. I was a TV talk show therapist analyzing Tim's best friend. He listened, seemingly interested.

"So what do I do?" he asked finally. "Do I call her on this last thing?"

"Sure you can, but she's not your problem. She does this to you twice a year and you always somehow put it behind you. We pray 'Bless them, change me.'" I reminded him of a story from an ancient Chinese Zen master, of the Buddha coming upon some people who had just been robbed while picnicking. They were racing around, enraged, asking him to help them. But Buddha asks, "Who would you rather find, the burglars or yourself?"

Tim nodded, and then said, "The burglars."

"Same."

We talked a bit more and then he packed up. I walked him to his car. As he left I stood waving beneath the bare witchy branches of the sycamore tree just outside our fence. Three branches angle up from its trunk and open way high up, punctuating the sky. They're so skinny but pretty damn strong: one long limb fell on our neighbor's car five years ago and smashed its roof in. I love the gray sky in between the branches—the subdued, the quietness—and how they reach upward like hands.

A few hours later as I settled in for a nap, my phone rang. It was Tim. His voice was tight and stricken. He said that he was sorry, but he didn't want me to be his mentor anymore. He said, "Listening to the cruel way you talked about Emma, I realized I don't want to turn out like you. You were so two-faced and mean."

I was struck by lightning, an electrical storm of shame, all but singeing my hair. I apologized profusely, and said I understood. The conversation took twenty seconds, and I was on the couch, alone in an empty house full of loud, shrill thoughts. I could have keened with mortification and the absolutely unshakable feeling that he was right. I was someone two-faced, and ugly on the inside, the worst thing a person can be in my book.

I might lose him, I thought, and on top of that, now everyone would find out. Tim and his wife would tell people in our community how I had harshed Emma. Someone once wrote that there is our public life, our private life, and our secret life, and my secret life now showed. It was like the gym in seventh-grade PE, all my shameful parts showing.

I cried.

Then, not knowing what else to do, I texted my girlfriend Janine. She called back. She is my PSS friend, Pray Share Shop (and some days my PSW, Pray Share Walk). I told her what Tim had said, and suggested I text him and beg for forgiveness. They say that in survival mode, there's fight, flight, or freeze, but there is a fourth possibility to which I frequently turn, and that is to fawn. My idea, my best thinking, was to fawn and debase myself. I asked Janine if it was okay to text Tim begging him to take me back.

"Maybe not today," she said, and asked if we

could pray for a moment. So I prayed with her, bitterly.

I was as afraid as a child. Deprived of the chance to grovel and win Tim back, I could not find a place to land. Tim was the one who saw the truth about me while other people, especially those who love me most, were somehow seduced by the Annie pheromones, or felt terribly sorry for me, or were obliged to stick around. My terror default from childhood was that critical people were right about my faults. They were being honest, not mean. Any meager good things about me paled in comparison, were outweighed by my character and personality disorders.

Tim had triggered the most universal fear: that once you really know us, we are not lovable.

When Neal finished work for the day, I told him what was going on. He was tender with me, mad at Tim, and went into caseworker mode. He made me a cup of tea and reminded me that I have an inner critic whose job is to keep me small and worried: Tim currently held its mic. This helped, but I still felt guilty, busted, and sad, just about as sorry as sheep shit.

The next morning I woke up anxious and de-pressed. I texted Janine: "Now can I text Tim and beg him to forgive me and take me back?"

"Maybe not today," she wrote back, a broken record playing for broken old me.

When broken is what we done got, where do we begin the repairs?

I wandered outside for fresh air. I wasn't in camellia mode; the blossoms seemed to be mocking me with their playfulness, or clueless to the point of unfeeling. There is a manzanita tree between the camellias and the fence and the wintry branches, lustrous with shiny red bark. Soon it would begin to grow new bark underneath the red layer, and as it shed, the red would peel off in thin crackling tubes, revealing baby green newness underneath. It's so satisfying to peel, like peeling your skin after a sunburn.

Damn! I thought I would grow out of this sensitivity someday, this super thin skin, but I haven't. I hated it as a little girl, I hate it as an older woman. Philip Roth told a young writer not to bank on getting thicker skin when the next book came out, or the one after that. "It'll get thinner and thinner," Roth said, "until they can hold you up to a light and see through." That's me. I tried to shake myself back into my essential wildebeest self, but all I felt was my butt swinging back and forth.

I put a bit of paper with Tim's initial on it in a tiny box where I give things to God when my own best thinking is making everything worse. I don't even know what it is I pray to sometimes—let's say to whatever made the trees and whatever beats my heart. I said to this power, "You think you're so big? Here, have a go at it."

Usually grace in its guise as spiritual WD-40 gets in and loosens the tight knot that has formed in the tangled gold chain of my best thinking. But not today.

I continued to fret as Neal made us a nice dinner and we binged on one of our dark Scandinavian thrillers that we find strangely calming. I read until late, slept, and was somewhat better the next morning, ten percent less desperate to call Tim and abase myself. I wrote down what terrible feelings and fears I was having about who I am deep down. I was told repeatedly as a child that I was too sensitive, that I took everything too seriously and too personally, and I said things without thinking. These remain true. My priest friend Terry Richie says we don't get over much here and I haven't. I still struggle with equal parts bad self-esteem and grandiosity. People tell me you have to reveal it to heal it, and I had, to Neal, Janine, and God; so where was the promised healing? I had to wonder if maybe I have too many bite marks on my soul's dorsal fins to ever feel free.

Janine called and ended up taking me for a walk in the woods. She went on and on about how neurotic Tim is, and how puzzling his devotion to bubbly unpleasant Emma is. She riffed on the weaponized breasts and the snakeskin purse. She was hilariously nasty, and it saved me.

Neal cooked again, and we watched the solemn and kind Norwegians duke it out with Albanian mobsters in a dark frozen wilderness. There is always some succor in how much worse things could be. At least I wasn't quite as morally bad as the men in the Albanian Mafia who were tormenting the nice Norwegians on TV. That's a start. Plus I reminded myself that I have a healthy body, a fine enough container for function, pleasure, pain, rest. These two attributes were huge. Before bed, I offered myself what I would offer any visitor: a hot bath, an apple, kind words, a good book.

The next day I texted Janine and asked if I could write Tim now and ask forgiveness if I promised not to grovel while pawing at the ground.

"Not today," she said again. "But I *will* authorize you to text yourself."

When all else fails, follow instructions, so I texted myself. I said I was so sorry for the shaming thoughts. I asked me on a date, for a walk, a trip to Target, and then a nap. I said yes. I was sad about

possibly losing Tim but was beginning to experience a return to my old self. The great universal
spirit always seems to tell me the same thing when
I am a mess and ask for help: You are not alone, Annie. Take gentle care. You are up to this, I promise.

And I always want to reply, Are you sure you
don't have me mixed up with someone else?

"Bless him, change me," was my prayer. Help
me like me again. Horrible Bonnie told me thirty
years ago when I was flattened in the aftermath
of a breakup, "Honey, you are preapproved." This
means in general, and if true I could live in that
preapproval, not Tim's ambush and judgment. My
thoughts turned to what it would be like the next
time Tim and I were in the same room together, if
he would look away and whisper to whomever he
was standing with. But I had apologized, expressed
contrition, surrendered, and asked God for help.
What was I supposed to do, put on a bejeweled jag-
uar mask and throw myself into a flaming pit? I
knew what Janine would say: "Maybe not today."

I did notice then that I was curious again, curious about what might happen next. When I first
got sober, a man told me that upon waking every
morning, instead of reciting the standard flowery
recovery prayer, he said, "Whatever," and at night
when he turned off his light to go to sleep, he said,

"Oh, well." In between he practiced simplicity—he stayed sober, worked on acceptance, tried to be of service to others, went for nature walks, picked up litter, made himself tea, and called it a day.

This is a perfect plan for living. My way, trying to nudge life and people into submission with my sensitivity and excellent ideas leaves me exhausted. The antidote is to surrender, lay down my sorry weapons and step over to the winning side, of friends, service, and fresh air. I opened the windows. I savor the fresh air whenever I remember to open them; the fresh air breathes the whole house.

I did exactly what the old timer said. Simplicity is such a beautiful way to live—and so not me. Whatever; sigh. I found a place to land, way down deep in the soft bullseye of me. Our innermost place is our shelter, what T. S. Eliot called "the still point of the turning world," and for the first time in days I found safety there.

What had happened? The thatched roof of me had blown off for a few days, and yet there I was, on a small plot of land inside, looking out at the passing scene, breathing. (You can never go wrong with breath.) I believe the Buddhists call this refuge. It was lovely, a one-woman nature preserve.

With no idea how things would shake down in my heart, I went outside. The early morning is

holy, forgiveness is holy, stopping to talk to neighbors is holy. I said hello to the camellias on the
way out. I was ready to make eye contact with
them again; they are sweet and friendly. More had
bloomed overnight, clownish but also elegant because of the pattern of the outer petals, tight and
rhythmical as artichokes. I said hello to the trees.
Hermann Hesse wrote, "Whoever has learned to
listen to the trees no longer wants to be a tree. He
wants to be nothing except what he is. That is
home. That is happiness." So I tried that on like a
flannel shirt.

And a few hours later Tim texted me, pouring
out his heart. He was so sorry for going off on me.
He had been wrong, such a jerk, always so overac-
tive, and plus, it had come out all wrong. He had
taken out his unhappiness with Emma and work
on me. He asked my forgiveness.

I said, "Hah! I don't want to turn out like *you*."

Not really. I said I loved him and I would never
mention Emma's name again as long as I lived.

He said—God is my witness—"Be my *guest*.
You won't believe what she said to Cory last night.
So thoughtless. I think you're right about the
jealousy . . ."

He went on and on. All I could do was hang my
head and smile. Then I looked up at the bush and

trees, fellow travelers, dying, shedding, blooming. The camellias are a little more blowsy every day. Their leaves are so glossy that they look laminated, as if they could withstand anything, including frost or wolf attack, as if they are saying to the flowers and the buds: We will protect you. Just grow. Be. Whatever.

THREE

Hinges

The back door creaked in the tiny house where I was conceived. Doors should not creak for many reasons, but mostly because that suggests the house is haunted. The creaky door in scary stories says there is someone nearby whom no one can see. Inside our house our creaky door spelled tension, but that same door led to a backyard world of tall grass, of bugs, worms, blackberries, butterflies, neighborhood children. My older brother and I used to barge out to freedom from the stresses and drinking inside, to sky and a view of the little white church on the hillside above us. The back door screen had torn from both bottom corners

and formed a sort of rusted wimple. In my excite-
ment to get out, I often scratched my legs on the
wire, and Dad would hammer it back into place,
and then it would pop back out at some point and
invariably lunge for my legs, as if trying to keep
me in.

My parents did not have loud fights, but they
were often to be found behind closed doors, my
mother sometimes crying because my father was
unhappy with her, my father hiding away peace-
fully in the alcove where he wrote, a cool refresh-
ing beer within reach.

I was five when my little brother was born.
There is a photo of the three of us kids on the
couch, my older brother and I both in fancy clothes
from Sears, my six-month-old brother in a onesie.
My big brother got to hold him because I'd been
crying. I cried in fear that the baby would die or my
parents would get divorced like Diane Henry's parents down the street. After the baby came, my father was often harsh with my mother, presumably
because she was still so heavy. My older brother and
I had to go through the kitchen to get to the back
door and she would be in there eating the homemade white bread she baked for us. My father loved
her cooking, but he watched her eat with contempt.

I dreamed of the baby drowning or being ab-

ducted. I remember that when I started crying that day, I'd been sent to the kitchen for the arti-choke jar.

If my older brother or I started to cry, unless we were hurt, we had to take the lid off an empty jar of marinated artichokes and cry into it. It was morti-fying, and I always hurt my bottom eyelid on the glass rim. I'm not sure where my parents had picked up this child-rearing tip or whether they had put their heads together one day and come up with it: "I know! If they must cry, we'll have them cry into artichoke heart jars."

"Excellent idea."

Despite such occasional lapses in judgment, they loved the three of us deeply. It was uncertain whether they cared for each other, and I took it upon myself to try to fill the holes this left them with. I got migraines. I washed my hands too often. I stood by my bedroom door every night at bedtime and turned the light switch on and off seventeen times, to stay safe. I spun on our rope swing until, climbing off, I staggered around joyfully.

I couldn't bear to see doors with ancient key-holes. They spelled death or imprisonment. Open doors, closed doors, wooden and glass, opaque, transparent. All doors spoke to me: enter, leave; invited, rejected. Mom's home, Dad has left again.

In 1960, when the baby was one and I was six, we moved to a dilapidated castle my parents bought for $20,000, a stone edifice a man had built for his Rhine-born wife in 1880, with thick stone walls, a dungeon, and caves in back. There were almost no doors when we moved in. My parents had a room at one end of the upstairs living area, and the three of us kids shared the rest of that cavernous space.

My mother sometimes slammed the bedroom door. A slam says, *I'm in here and I'm shutting you out and you can't come in;* it was door as a symbol of aggression. The opposite was the wondrous portal downstairs, the door to my dad's study. He closed the door behind him at 5:30 a.m. five days a week. We woke up every weekday morning to him tap-tap-tapping at his heavy black Olympia typewriter. You knocked on the door's glass panes for admission. Inside he was god, a pasha in an L.L. Bean chamois shirt, surrounded by walls of books, some of which he'd written.

There were old white hinges on the door with flecks of rust that he meant to get to.

Hinges: that word lives inside me. A hinge both fixes something in place and helps it open. It's ingenious. A hinge has the feeling for me of a book opening, welcoming me in, closing a while later with a soft sigh. Without a hinge, doors can't swing.

Behind his office door I became the girl my father adored, who could read books meant for much bigger kids and talk about them in a way that pleased him. I had gotten funny as a first line of defense against getting bullied in school, and I could make him laugh. He gave me pictures and told me to write about them as I sat on the floor with my back against his bookshelves. He taught me how to compute on an abacus, which he'd grown up using in Tokyo, and on a slide rule, which he used in engineering school at Yale before he switched to English. He taught me algebra years before I would need it just because it was sort of fun. He taught me how to do research in the big brown single-volume *Columbia Encyclopedia*, the '60s fount of all truth and knowledge.

Outside the study, my mother grew heavier and my father spent more time in his office or having drinks with his writer friends. There were other women. My mother valiantly, grimly, tried to improve the marriage. One afternoon when my little brother was three, there was a knock on the downstairs door and through the six panes, I could see my mother standing on the other side, almost unrecognizable and beaming shyly. She had spent the day in San Francisco at Elizabeth Arden's Maine Chance salon, getting her long beautiful black hair cut off and styled, wearing foundation and sky-blue eyeshadow, all in an effort to win back my father.

My little brother wandered by and threw himself into my arms crying because he didn't know who she was, and here she wanted to scoop him up in a hug. My father looked at her with mild curiosity. "Hmmm," he said. "Wow." Then he made her an old-fashioned: sugar, bitters, bourbon, with a maraschino cherry, and that was the end of that.

Some of my best girlhood friends lived in big fancy houses with brass knockers on the front door. I felt this indicated good character and believed that if we had one, our family would be happier. I had bad door self-esteem.

I would sit behind Dad's closed study door with him and we would talk about books and science. Every so often we'd hear my mother slam the door upstairs, because she was English and thus not allowed to express pain or say she wished she had a hand grenade. The slammed door said, *I am in so much pain and no one cares.* When she came out again, she would take us in her arms.

Only inches thick, but what a complex barrier a

door can create in your life. When my older brother and I were twelve and ten, my dad took a job as a planning consultant for medical schools in downtown Tiburon to cover our growing expenses. We would drop by after school to hit him up for money to get snacks on our way home. He shared a large office with an attractive woman slightly younger than he was who was the exact opposite of my mother—trim, coiffed, fashionable. She wore sleek black eyeliner. I could tell they both loved it when I stopped by as I offered an adorable, chatty, fawning break in their routine. Bonnie was smitten with me, as were all of Dad's friends. Charm was my superpower. Then he'd give me a quarter for a candy bar.

This went on for years. Dinners at home were chilly, and as time passed doors slammed more often. I did what I could to smooth out everyone's feelings, making drop-in therapy visits to each individual behind whatever closed door they had found refuge. The next day, I'd stop by Dad and Bonnie's office for a chat that left him beaming with pride, although rather early on in all this I'd raised my price to a buck.

I learned that my father had stormed out of the castle and his twenty-seven-year marriage one night when I was away at college. He fled to our tiny cabin on the coast—to freedom, to Bonnie. Five years later, when I was twenty-three, he got brain cancer. The night he died, my brothers and his best friend followed his body outside behind the coroner's gurney. My older brother took off his own watch and put it on my father's wrist. The two men from the mortuary closed the door of their van in almost perfect silence.

Seven drunken, stoned years after he died, I stood outside a door at a church on a hill in Sausalito, trying to work up my courage. The red door had an arch at its top. An arch says welcome. An arch says a little bit of holy. Inside was a nightmare waiting for me, thirty or forty sober alcoholics under fluorescent lights, drinking the swill that passed for coffee before the revolution of the late '80s. But I had been visited by grace in its distressing guise of having run out of any more good ideas. I stepped through the arch into the fluorescent lighting.

Miracles rarely are lovely: a door opens and you go through, and God is not waiting there squealing with delight to see you, with leis and cranberry spritzers. You enter and you can't even tell what you are seeing but you do know it is not good. People seemed to want to help me get sober, which was not what I wanted. I wanted to learn to stop after six or seven nightly social drinks. I wanted to wake up without hangovers. I wanted to be a person of integrity. I wanted all that, and a nice cool drink.

I walked to a table and sat down. I hated the hour I spent there, especially that I identified with every speaker; hated the women who came up to me like cheerleaders and gave me their phone numbers. But as I said, I had run out of good ideas. This is often necessary for grace to appear. Also, there were cookies. I hated it less and less over the next couple of months as I went back, and then I fell in love with it.

Getting and staying sober was the hardest work I'd ever done. I was scared and ashamed, defeated and defiant. Yet what those people gave me, and continue to give me decades later, remains the great gift and miracle of my life. They gave me *me*, they gave me a way of life, they gave me everything alcohol had promised. All miracles begin with a hopeless mess or bad news, and that was me, Exhibit A.

In the movies, when God and Moses part the Red Sea, the Israelites skip across the dry sand to the land of milk and honey. But actually it must have been terrifying. There was a parting of the waves, an opening through the sea that had been peeled back on both sides, towering and thunderous, and most of those people must have been shaking as they tried to get to the other side. The moms clutching their babies, the elderly on crutches or on their grown sons' backs, little children weeping as the walls of seawater trembled above them. The path would have been slimy with algae, tiled with broken shells and bones that cut one's feet. But they kept going until they reached wilderness on the other side.

Wilderness waited for me on the other side of the arched door. I'm here to tell you that wilderness sucks. I muddled through memories of childhood, of my parents' unhappy life at the castle. I learned to take basic care of myself and I took care of my mother. I helped her do errands, I brought her lunch, watched tennis on TV with her. She was a handful of needs, complaints, and weirdness. I was gentle with her, but when I got back to my car, I would rest my forehead against the steering wheel.

Love is patient and kind and sometimes looks like a well-meaning person gripping their forehead like a vise, and keening.

Then one morning in late 1988 the man I had been dating exclusively for six months stood outside the door of the studio apartment I was renting in the redwoods. There were clear glass panels in the white door, and I could see that he looked grim.

I welcomed him in and set about trying to help him feel better. What I didn't know was that he had come by to tell me that another woman was going to be moving in with him soon, a woman he had forgotten to mention who was ten years younger than I was, who wore miniskirts and a leather jacket. But he never got around to telling me that day because I made him feel so much better that I ended up pregnant.

He did mention when I walked him to the door that he was going to be busy with a project for a while and wouldn't be able to see me as much, and I thought: *Hey, no biggie, right?* I was just so pleased that I had cheered him up.

He went crazy when he discovered I was keeping the baby, what with his cute new roommate, and then he slammed the door on us for the next seven years.

With no man and no money, love pushed back its sleeves and took over. We were provided with everything we needed, and then some. People arrived every day at that white-paned door with food, diapers, ice cream bars. My mother and my aunt Pat came over twice a week and physically fought for possession of the baby. I got therapy to learn to let people take care of *me*. What a concept. Love poured over me, into me, under me, buoying me up. It was a little hard to take, but I had no choice.

Sam was a heartbreakingly lovely little person and then, like me, he grew up to be a teenager who loved to drink and smoke dope, and over time he also discovered meth. We were both going nuts, so I got him his own apartment twenty minutes away. A beautiful girl moved in with him and got pregnant a year later. They were both nineteen. I rented them an apartment in San Francisco near where he worked, and they had a baby boy. I got to see the baby every few days and sometimes overnight. When they weren't getting along, they confided in me. But when they were loving each other, I got shut out or put down so I was back on the triangle of a beloved man, a beleaguered woman, and me. Ah, home sweet home.

I swallowed any bad feelings that arose until eventually they backed up into my throat, and then I would call Horrible Bonnie, my mentor of thirty-five years, who dresses like it's still the '60s. Although I adore her, I've always called her Horrible Bonnie because she lives in hope and optimism as a decision, no matter what fresh hell has appeared or been elected. She always listens, cooing, then points out to me that I seem once again to be trying to help crazy hostile people feel good about their lives. So who was the crazy one? She'd remind me of a pin I used to wear that said, "It's not them," which I believe about half the time. We'd end up laughing and I'd be better for a time, until the cycle started up again. Stuff, implode, call Bonnie. Stuff, implode, call Bonnie.

Things deteriorated between Sam and Amy, so I invited her and the toddler to move in with me. It was hard and Sam was going down the tubes and I had to ask him not to come to the house unless he was clean and sober. The door reverberated when he slammed it. Horrible Bonnie said this was excellent news—my healthy boundary, his worsening condition. (See why I call her that?) I needed to put Sam in God's good hands, she'd say, and retire as his higher power. So I did. And one day he called to say he had ten days sober and all these sober men in San Francisco were helping him under bad lights with great coffee. Could he come see us all?

God, yes. Run.

An hour later I opened the big red splintered door to my prodigal son and welcomed him home. That was September 6, 2012. Amy and the child moved out a few months later, but I still made sure neither she nor Sam had a moment's displeasure that might cause Sam to get drunk and stoned again. It was exhausting. I walked on eggshells, not wanting to say the wrong thing, and listened to them complain about each other. Good old me.

Then on one particularly bad day, when my older brother happened to be staying with me, Sam and Amy both criticized me by phone over the course of an hour, darling obsequious me. My brother saw me tearing up and asked if I wanted to talk. He, as a born-again Christian, had some corrective thoughts on how I should feel. I love him so much, but what he had to offer felt like patronizing Christian bumper stickers: God never gives us more than we can bear, and everything happens for a reason. I felt that he might be about to try and get me to join him in singing "Jesus Wants Me for a Sunbeam." And then I'd have to attack him. I stutter-stepped away and said I'd suddenly remembered that I had to do some errands. He looked puzzled. I got the car keys and raced out the door.

I barely made it to the car before I started sobbing. I slammed the car door and started shouting at the top of my lungs about how much I hated everyone: my son, Amy, even my poor brother. Then as I drove along, ugly crying, I turned on my mother and father, whom I had also taken such good care of, for the horrible models of so-called love they'd offered their kids. I shouted at my dad that I hated him for how he treated Mom, and I shouted at my mom for not leaving him, and I shouted at the two of them that their contempt for each other had bathed us in pressure and self-loathing, since we couldn't make them happier. I drove out to the country, shouting at the top of my lungs, something I had never done before *in my life.*

I turned around at some point and drove back past the golden hills, the fields filled with cows and lambs, the redwoods and eucalyptus, and by then I had stopped shouting because I was losing my voice but kept on crying. Finally I pulled over in front of the post office, turned off the car engine, and called Horrible Bonnie.

"Oh, dearest," she said, hearing my hoarse and tearful voice. "Talk to me." I let it all pour out: the exhaustion of trying so hard, of being taken advantage of, of not being anyone's priority, of hating them all, of my deep, deep loneliness.

When I finally stopped, there was silence. Then she said: "This is what we paid for all these years. I am thanking God, Annie; you've got your foot in the door."

Oh, stop, I thought. For Pete's sake. How could that possibly be? But she went on. The reason I was nobody's priority was that I wasn't my own and never had been. It was time to lavish on myself the kind of focused care and affection I shone on everyone else.

Red, snotty, and swollen, I had no fight left in me. So I listened. She said she had been exactly where I was now with her own grown kids, and *her* spiritual mentor had suggested that she practice being her own romantic partner. It had made her sick to her stomach and confused at the time, and yet it changed her life forever.

Sick to my stomach and confused, I told her I wouldn't even know where to start. Do I get myself a corsage? Make myself a baked Alaska?

"Yes on the corsage," she said, "or at least some flowers." After a few sullen moments of silence, I agreed to do that.

"And stop holding your neck out for them to feed on. Start saying "No" more often when they want something. No is a complete sentence. And remember: it's not them."

Well, I wouldn't go that far. It kind of *was* them. But putting that aside, I bought myself flowers, got some homemade tamales for dinner, and headed home.

"Do you still want to talk?" my brother asked when I stepped through the door.

God, no. I'd experienced such release that I couldn't risk any more Christian uplift. I just wanted him to binge on old episodes of *The Bob Newhart Show* with me, not have any interesting opinions about me, and share a massive bowl of popcorn. And he did. That is what love looks like.

I did this radical self-love every day for a few months, and then Neal basically fell through the door. The door and I had been waiting for him, for this one exact guy I now get to wake up with every morning.

I don't know how that happened and I don't know what will happen down the road, but as Neal said once, "I don't know" is a portal.

"I don't know" is also a hinge.

The front door of our new house is tomato-soup red with a lot of square panels, like windows that aren't. We got it at a junkyard. It has a viewer like a door in a medieval castle so you can open the window and look out through a grate at whoever knocks, to make sure it is not Visigoths or Witnesses. The tiny window is textured goldenrod plastic. The hinges are old and beginning to rust. The door might need a little WD-40, but who doesn't? Neal switched out the door's other hardware for elegant brushed nickel, and screwed in metal plates at the base both inside and out because the dogs scratch at the door to come in and go out, come in and go out, all day. Before that, they had eaten a corner of the door and badly scratched the jamb. What kind of being eats their own front door? It's those who think that doors shouldn't even be there. "Why do you want to keep us out? Why do you want to keep us in?"

Our door protects us, and from inside we can look out through the yellow window at the world, at the wind tossing the branches of our trees, the leaves fluttering and talkative. Our door is pretty banged up, peculiar and beautiful—sort of like me—and behind it, watching all of life go by, I finally feel safe.

FOUR

Minus Tide

Sometimes it all just sucks, as Jesus says somewhere in the Gospels (although off the top of my head I can't recall chapter and verse). Life becomes a lava lamp of memories of happier and sadder times, of what might have been, and of a fearful future, accompanied by the burbling sound of advancing time, of which one friend has almost run out, and of which I will too someday (supposedly).

It's a ten-minute walk to where my friendship with Karen Carlson took off, twenty-six years ago at the trailhead in Deer Park. She used to lead a group of us, all older than she was, up and down the wooded trails, alternately jogging and walking

fast. She called it "scampering" and inducted us
into the International Order of the Squirrel, Local
37. I still have my squirrel keychain. After she'd
had her dominatrix way with us, she'd race off
alone for a five-mile run, uphill, which struck us
all as an act of aggression, as we stood around,
hands on our hips, heaving for breath. Now Karen
can hardly breathe.

I do not agree to this turn of events, partly because it makes no sense. (I think we can all agree
that life should make more sense.) For a long time
after Karen's diagnosis of hypersensitivity pneu-
monitis and through a harrowing double lung
transplant, I was pissed off.

But lately a dark beauty has made itself known.

I first met Karen when she was a trainer at a
women's gym in town, which I had joined in the
hopes of firming up the jiggly bits, especially the
cellulite on the back of my thighs and the catastrophe of my upper arms. She was very funny, brilliant, and highly educated, and turned out to be
the only person I've ever known who is a worse
know-it-all than my husband. I think she alone
could have beaten him at Scrabble, and I'm glad
she didn't as this would have killed him, rendering
him useless to me.

Now she cannot get out of bed except for trips

to the city for last-ditch treatments that can pro-
long but not improve her life. She has three beautiful grandchildren nearby, so it's nearly impossible
for her to accept her impending death. Those damn
grandchildren ruin everything.

I tell her there is a heaven, and she pats me like
I am a sweet little dog.

I haven't seen her for two weeks because I have
COVID, but I still drop off orange Jell-O and vanilla pudding cups, which is what she is living
on now.

I asked her five years ago when the disease was
first detected how this could possibly have happened. It meant to me that life makes no sense. She
said, "This happens to people, and I am a person."
My response was to itemize truly detestable people
who it should have happened to if, again, life made
sense.

Literally nothing works in her life and body
anymore, except her mind and her heart. Every
human thing about her is exposed: her longing to
live, her powerlessness, her passionate love of her
kids and grandkids and a few friends.

I've come to see her as an extreme minus tide,
the kind I grew up seeing every year as a child
playing in West Marin tide pools, when the ocean
has rolled way back toward the horizon, and the

sand is stretched out over where the water used to be like a drum skin, covered with boulders, algae, and every form of marine life. She tried to drag me to one last summer, when she could still get around. I didn't go that time because you had to get up at four a.m. and I had been traveling a lot, was too tired, and had seen it many times over the years. Four years younger than I, she seemed suddenly ten years older but still got up several times in the very, very early morning to go with other friends to see what is submerged 353 days of the year.

At the time, Karen had the expectation of living at least another five or six years. Her courage over the three years of sometimes unbelievable suffering and pain was heroic. She was matter-of-fact about new problems and surgeries. Her stamina and commitment were amazing, the pain crankily tolerable. But right after those minus tides, her body went into a sudden and precipitous decline, the kind where hopelessness can set in.

As civilized people, we rarely notice how our will to live, our love of life—no matter how hard it can be—pulses inside of us. We are so busy; we have our families, to-do lists, fixations, strivings. Our will to live, our life force, gets submerged under thoughts, busyness, regrets, ambition. But

Karen noticed. She made her friends walk with her for miles and miles to keep her lungs functioning, and because the outdoors is her heaven on Earth. And little by little the walks grew shorter and then she couldn't walk at all.

Love of life? Oh, sure, we feel it when we're in love, while waiting for biopsies, while playing with Neal's marvelous granddaughter in Chicago, on tropical vacations. But I lost this love when I got COVID for the second time and had to cancel a spiritual retreat in Maui. I had the decency not to bring up my disappointment with Karen, but I was so bummed that I called my Jesuit friend Tom to complain.

"Life just totally sucks today. Doesn't Jesus say that somewhere? I'm supposed to be on a plane to Hawaii. But instead I'm sick as a dog."

"Oh no, one of my roommates had that again, too. We voted not to shoot him, after a lengthy discussion," Tom said.

"Will you give me last rites?"

Neal chimed in before Tom could answer. "Can you wait on this? I haven't gotten all I need out of her yet."

Tom said, "We can give you twenty-four hours, Neal."

This is how the people in my world handle death, with lots of banter and black humor, but when Tom dies, I will want to give up for a long time. And he will never get over my death, never stop hating that I have died, which is how I want it to be for those who love me, some days. (Well, most days.)

"Can you really give a Protestant last rites?" I asked.

"Yes," he said, "if they are pathetic enough."

My brothers and I used to be able to walk to the minus tide beach with our dad when we were young, from a one-room cabin my grandparents owned, but it is nearly an hour away by car from where we live now. To get there, you drive past a glorious landscape, hills like lionesses above farmland with furrowed fields, green pastures, and cows. To see an extreme minus tide, you leave in the dark, the moon still high but the world starting to be light as you drive. You can just make out nocturnal animals along the road—skunks, coyotes, fortunate kitty cats heading home after a long night at the office. In the trees surrounding the parking lot at the beach are a lot of owls nesting loudly in the trees.

The light is not to be believed, the dawn's light you also get at dusk, the light all the cinematographers wait for. You walk from the parking lot down along a riparian corridor, an underground river that you can't see but can tell is there because willows and cottonwood trees and vegetation have sprung up over it, saying, "Water, water, fresh water, step right up." Rabbits scatter from the path ahead.

My father would get the three of us up way before dawn for these extreme minus tides. The heightened bird activity alone meant everything to him, a lifelong bird-watcher, because so many gulls and black oystercatchers descended from the sky, looking like a fantastic mobile over the sumptuous low tide spread, while egrets and great blue herons stood watching sanctimoniously. Bird-watching was my father's religion, the reef and the hiking trails on Mount Tamalpais his church, finches and sparrows his cantors. One morning not too long before he died, his girlfriend and my younger brother and I took him to the tide pools one morning. He was fifty-six, eight years younger than Karen. I have a photograph of him in a navy blue knit cap and the iconic L.L. Bean Norwegian fisherman's sweater he had been ordering since they first came out. He clutched his walking stick and stood next to a tide pool, smiling broadly, as if about to raise his arms before the rising sun.

Huge craggy rock formations, usually sub-merged under the chilly Pacific Ocean, are revealed

during these tides. Some are long like crocodile
snouts, some tall as dinosaurs, each with many different textures and shades, detailed and nuanced as
a William Morris woodcut. They're covered with
mussels, barnacles, periwinkles, and mollusks of
all kinds. Below, the rocky pools between them are
filled with seaweed and look like giant soup tu-
reens. Alien life-forms scuttle through the algae.
There are zebra-striped keyhole limpets, chitons,
more mussels and barnacles, snails, and many kinds
of anemones, some with an inside that looks like
the skin on a lime, others the exact color of saltwa-
ter taffy. They attract all kinds of detritus, so they
are speckled and spangled with broken shells and
stones. They're both armored and wide open at the
same time like the best of us. As you wander farther out toward the horizon, there are hundreds of
enormous starfish—bigger than dinner plates because they are very old—bright orange, pink and
lilac, and some combos, like a bleed in your rain-
bow sherbet.

The hermit crabs are the comic relief. They
come scurrying out of the crevices, using their
claws for balance as they run down the sides of
rocks, waving their claws in the air like the cranky
old man down the street of your childhood, and

they get in fights with each other. It's theater of the absurd in miniature, like clown fights at a rodeo.

Farthest out in the deepest pools where the ocean finally meets the reef, there is a species of small octopus in pink chiffon who looks just like Zsa Zsa Gabor.

When I was small, a very low tide looked like another world, like the surface of a watery planet. In summer, the hills above it hold this beach in their camel-colored arms.

On this day, when we didn't know he only had a few more months to live, I remember my dad slipping on the algae and falling on his butt. It took both of his grown kids to get him back to his feet. He was like one of those small disjointed push puppets on a stand, whose base you pressed to cause its collapse. Dad's pants got wet, but he was just happy to be on the reef with us, a part of the whole, the ocean, his family, morning, the tide pools just after sunrise. We all felt it, that rare feeling, those moments out of time, not religious or esoteric, just piercingly alive for a few moments, moments of eternity, my father tasting the joy of being alive.

"Death, where is thy sting-a-ling-a-ling?" went an old song from World War I that cheered the troops as they marched, one of the military songs that my father and his drinking buddies sang along with the Field Artillery song—over hill, over dale, etc. They had all fought in World War II and taught their children the military cadence calls. Fight, fight, fight.

That day on the reef there was no sting, no cancer, no fight, just simply the day's own self.

Once Karen looked up to the hillside above the reef and found it lined with coyotes like in the old cowboy movies. I once saw a bobcat halfway up the hill and prepared to fight it off with my bare hands, but thankfully, like most bobcats encountering humans, it skulked up the hill. It knew it wouldn't have stood a chance against me.

Twenty-two years ago when I confessed to Karen at the gym that I was tormented by the disappointing condition of my upper arms, she made me a tiny book with index cards stapled together, called *Annie's Beautiful Arms*. Inside were stamp-size pictures of the arms of Venus on the clamshell, young prince Siddhartha, a chubby baby, and mine. It was like the books we used to make our parents when we were kids. I still have it and I still have her and I need to remember that.

We've sat in dry sand and stared out at the ocean here. I don't know what makes some of the water leap up out there in that broad indigo ocean like little white dolphins. When the tide is in, the reef is lacy with water rolling back and forth, sculptural, a bas-relief. The air here is a cocktail of native plants, marine life, soil, and algae, and no matter what time of day, the dampish dewy smell of morning.

The tide comes in, the tide goes out, and when you are older, around the time when you stop feeling like you've crawled into somebody else's shell, old friends begin to die with appalling regularity. If life made sense, they would all be older when they went. How did they get old enough to die? My father's death feels like it was twenty years ago but it was more than forty-five. It races, like scrolling through microfiche, *zzzzzip*, and nothing anyone says can make this less awful. Well, maybe one thing: Kitty Carlisle's mother said the good thing about being older is that every fifteen minutes, it's time for breakfast again. Karen has tea, an Oxy-Contin, and orange Jell-O for breakfast now.

She is so sick and sad that it can be hard to be with her, but until I got COVID recently, I showed up and listened. Most of the time that is all we have to offer, and it is enough. Come to think of it, it was also hard in its own way to be with her many times over the years because she can be a curmudgeon and contrarian. Plus, horribly for me, her three grown kids, who are all pretty amazing, were also extreme achievers, which my son Sam was not. All those years until 2012 when my son got clean and sober, she and I would be on a trail at Deer Park and she'd tell me all about the grad schools her kids had graduated from or just been admitted to, and then ask what Sam was up to.

"Ah, well, still living in the Tenderloin," I'd say, a young father, scaring us all to death. But he was alive—I was one of the lucky ones, and I knew that, and this gave me a shaky hope. But I lived in the minus tide of long-term fear, where most of life's safety and predictability seemed to have been sucked away to unknown places. All I had throughout were my friends and faith that the tide would come in again.

The worst phase was one year when Karen's son was in medical school, and she rejoiced in recounting the details of his summer job as a runway model in Milan. She'd asked what Sam had been up to. He was at his lowest point—we both were—but he did have a decent job and a wonderful girlfriend and so I ran with that. Then when grace beckoned to Sam and lured him back and into the company of some sober guys in San Francisco, I got to tell her the minutiae of our miracle, and she cried with relief for me and we got to be two proud braggy mothers.

It is so hard for Karen to stay alive right now, and we both know she is about to die, but when I pay attention, I see that this takes a back seat to her being alive, stroking the luxurious fur of her cat, sipping her tea with a best friend, watching videos of her grandchildren. And her face brightens when she sees me; her light is still on in there, like a nightstand lamp between those dark, dangerous lungs.

Sometimes when I sit with her on her bed, memories float up to her of our earliest adventures that I've forgotten. Doing the Banana Dance twenty-five years ago to accompany our folk singer friend at a bookstore whose carpet was tiled in young children, singing along to the song of the same name. Scantily dressed, we were a couple of foxes shimmying. Oh, did we peel. And another memory: When I helped out at the dance classes she held for developmentally disabled adults every Tuesday for years, one young man told her later: "I liked that girl. She was a helper, and she danced." This will be in the swag bag of general instructions I leave behind for my grandson when I'm gone. Be a helper, and dance.

The small walk-in closet in Karen's hilariously

tiny apartment is stuffed with clothes and shoes, heavy on Doc Martens. Recently while instructed to move things around in the hopes of locating a clean tube for her emergency oxygen machine, I found two heavy winter coats. I said, "Do you want to give one away?" She doesn't: It's been freezing and she doesn't know which one she'll be in the mood for the next time she goes in for treatment, the dark gray one or the navy blue. I love that so much.

It now takes friends an hour to help her get awake, dressed, and down a flight of stairs, and the whole time she's in pain and gasps for breath.

The other day when I talked to Tom about how some days everything sucks, his roommate, another Jesuit, was listening on speakerphone and called out, "Yes, Jesus was full of compassion for those suffering, but also says to look for hope one day at a time, to see that if the lilies of the field and the sparrows were cared for, how much more would we be?"

"That's very nice, Jim. It would be easy if you were a bird or plant," I countered.

"You have a choice," he said. "What are you going to focus on, Annie?" he asked. "All the things that suck, or sparrows and lilies?"

I thought this over. "Can I get back to you on that?" As I've said before, I have a PhD in morbid reflection, and in a strange way it centers me.

Karen loves to look through photos in her albums and on her laptop. The last time we were together, she showed me photographs of the last extreme minus tide. Looking at the pictures, you can't help but wonder where all that water goes. It looks as if it has all been sucked up in a great inhalation by a sea monster; what if she gets sick of the routine and expels it all at once, causing a tsunami, burying this gorgeous tidal creation and darling me? Will these tide pools disappear forever someday as the sea levels rise? Luckily, I suppose, we'll be gone, but our grandchildren won't and this shakes me to my core.

I scare myself with recreational morbidity by wondering when will my last day come, and if I will be very afraid. But these are the wrong questions to ponder. Watching Karen, the question is how do you notice your own life force now?

She has a photo of herself with a walking stick on the reef at the last minus tide. She's smiling. She was always beautiful and loved that about

herself—she'd been a model as a young woman—
and now she looks rather like some sherpa's favorite
grandmother in her wool cap and layers of warmth.
What brought her here to this point? Well, what
brought any of us here with her? An unimaginably
complex and infinite number of intergenerational
variables that made her specifically herself. The
theologian Frederick Buechner wrote: "The grace
of God means something like: 'Here is your life.
You might never have been, but you *are*, because
the party wouldn't have been complete without
you.'" Being at all, living, is a miracle, and—note to
self—attention must be paid.

Karen started planning a party on the beach a
couple of weeks ago. She called it her last hurrah, a
wake to be held while she was alive, with a few of
us in the sand with torches, barbecue, singing, she
in a wheelchair that can travel in sand. But then
the rains came and the party has been postponed.
I'd give almost anything to sit with her in the sand
one more time.

I have been with many people who were dying,
and what is revealed besides the worry is all that
they loved, both what they will miss and what still
fills and feeds them. Karen in bed with her cat and
us, photos of her family; my father happy as a child
that last morning on the beach, wet pants and all.

Those ornate ordinary times, the grip of a hand as you walk up the trail to the car, laughing in spite of it all, vanilla pudding.

I show up, and Karen and I look at things together. Sometimes we make each other laugh. Her imagination is intact, as are her flights of fancy and her glorious plans for revenge. I make her tea with sugar. When I last saw her, she told me a story about how once when she and her son were about to head back to the car from the tide pools, they saw a coyote come trotting out of the chaparral and run down to the beach, frolicking in the water, running in and out of the foam at the shore, the way you would if you were a dog, or a kid, as my brothers and I did when we were small, as some children will almost certainly do later today when the tide is in. Talk about the joy of living. Talk about life making sense.

FIVE

Somehow

We humans screw up; that is our nature. Francis Spufford wrote in his book *Un-apologetic* that the human propensity is to fuck things up. There is a flaw in our genetic and social coding, which is why we keep kicking up errors in the form of damage to our relationships, to ourselves, and to the planet. Most of the blame goes to the ego, protecting and promoting itself without a thought for the neighbor, the community, the divine. It is always trying to get away with more, while obsessing about how unfair it is that others get away with so much. It's the part of me that always wants the bigger cookie and glares at someone else if they take it before I can. It's the part of me that would have me pushing aside women even older than I am to get to the *Titanic* lifeboats.

To make this flaw worse, some of us grew up in families where mistakes felt like matters of life and death, where you might get the belt or sent to your room without eating (as in my family), which bred the sickness of perfectionism and a lifelong fear of making mistakes, especially in public. But committing a public disgrace is exactly what I did this one time. And it was truly reprehensible.

Most mistakes we make are of almost no consequence and cause only passing embarrassment, while others are far more dramatic, perhaps especially the ones some of us made as parents, which we grieve for the rest of our lives. But this one caused actual pain to a lot of innocent people.

I have written elsewhere that many years ago I trashed the world's most famous transgender person by retweeting an extremely offensive joke that a dear friend had tweeted. I cannot stomach hurting people, and that was the worst part and my biggest regret. And it was a soul-tearing experience to find myself in the role of bigot when I've fought my whole life against bigotry. But is bringing it up again beating a dead horse? No—the horse just turned out to be playing possum.

At the time, nearly ten years ago, the tweet went viral, I was chastised in the media, my son turned on me, and I did everything possible to make amends. I wrote a long and entirely contrite essay in a book. I steered clear of the obvious excuses. I bared my soul. I groveled. I crawled. I felt shitty. I did as much as I could do. And then, because life has to go on, I laid it to rest.

But surprise, surprise, not everyone did.

I was invited to give the commencement address at a Catholic college graduation by video, as COVID raged. I wrote a fifteen-minute talk hitting on all my deepest beliefs, mostly that these newly launched bachelors of science and the arts could trust in the goodness of God, no matter what it looked like, no matter how long it took. That the respect they were desperate for was not out there, it was an inside job. That they were obviously exhausted and were invited to lie down in green pastures. That what their butts looked like was number 137 on the list of what matters in life. Once again. Whenever they wanted to have loving feelings, all they needed was to do loving things— magic. And that, as Saint Paul said, you're alive if you love the brothers and sisters. Otherwise, there's just death.

The chair of the humanities department and

two graduates from the technology program came to my house to record it. The chair and I had a lovefest. One of the students teared up.

Four days later, my agent called to say that three students had gone to the dean of the college to protest my having been chosen as their commencement speaker, what with—and I quote—my "history of transphobia." The speech was being canceled, as was I. A new speaker was selected. This was horribly embarrassing, but child's play compared to what happened the next day: The dean of the college sent a letter to the students, their parents, thousands of alumni, and, to make it even more festive, the media. She took responsibility for having inadvertently agreed to have someone with a history of transphobia as the college's commencement speaker and assured her audience that she would do everything in her power to protect the student body going forward.

When I make a significant mistake with someone, I slide down the shame spiral. It feels like I have pulled out the wrong block at Jenga and everything crashes to the ground, most painfully my sense of self-worth. So when the dean sent her letter, my sin was revealed for all to see, and people got to talk about it among themselves.

Neal did all the right things to see me through—namely, coddled me and disparaged the dean, even though he doesn't think that mistakes are actually mistakes. He believes that landing someplace awful gives us a new starting point for our journeys and the chance to see that we are deeply, simply human. He makes this sound like a good thing, the opportunity to experience our very ordinary and most vulnerable moments, in gratitude that we are fed, clothed, warm, and loved and that there are no muggers or snakes in the room. If we were still a tribal people we'd be leaning back from the table, telling jokes and stories of the ancestors. But we aren't. And I hate it.

When we screw up or even sin in the archery sense of the word—when we miss the target—it is never the final word. The fact that this happens to all of us allows us to have a tenderness about the broken places. We are all hopelessly stuck with being human. But our having messed up stops running our lives as much when we "call a thing what it is," as Luther put it. This actually offers us a place of hope, the hope of relaxing about our brokenness to some degree, whereas pretending it's not like this will never save us.

I have stated elsewhere that hope is believing

this one thing, that love is bigger than any grim, bleak shit anyone can throw at us. And I believe.

Also, my experience is that grace bats last, and after the dean's letter appeared in the local news-papers, half a dozen beloved writers stepped up and wrote stern letters to the dean and the media attesting to my goodness and generosity. There was an outpouring of affirmation and affection, and I lurched through the next few weeks on this love and on my favorite emotional response of all, victimized self-righteousness.

Apricity means the warmth of the sun in win-ter, and the warmth for me was people loving on me out loud. It streamed through me, because the exposure and talking it over with friends had made me so permeable. I learned—once again—that just about the worst part about shame is the shame of still having it. But the willingness to change and grow comes from the pain of stagnation. Robert-son Davies, the brilliant Canadian author of the Deptford Trilogy, describes a medical process from the days before antibiotics called laudable pus, when the only option a doctor had to heal someone with an old and imperfectly healed wound was to lance it. He would slice as deeply as he could with his scalpel until he could make an opening in the area where the pus had collected so that it could get out.

Then the wound could be flushed with water, alcohol, and tinctures, and heal from deep inside. This is what healing felt like, disgusting and cleansing.

I dusted myself off: thank God that stupid thing had been laid to rest. We open our wounds when we are finally able so they can be healed from inside out, and close.

If I can get word to my grandson from the other side when I am gone, I will whisper to him when he is in trouble to make a gratitude list—no snakes in the room, yay!—then do his chores, be kind to himself, be of service, get outside, and breathe. This is the launch code when under attack: gratitude, chores, chocolate, service, breath, nature.

Back when I was dealing with my unfortunate retweeting, I went for longer walks every day for a while. A ten-minute walk from my house brings me to the grove where my brothers and I scattered our mother's ashes in a glade ringed with eucalyptus trees. This is a sacred clearing. The scent of camphor is medicinal. It reminds me of rosemary and it spritzes me back to the now. The long trunks are like organ pipes, so stately, so erect, so exquisitely spaced. Each has its own tone, yet they are joined in an upright community.

Rumi said that through love, all pain will turn to medicine, and I did the work until the mess turned into a story I could tell, in which people recognized themselves and laughed. From time to time, the memory would surface along with flickers of shame, and when that happened I relied on the protocol: gratitude, chores, chocolate, service, breath, nature. My progressive Catholic friend Sara Miles tells people, when they are tweaking and ob-sessing, "Oh, the Boyfriend is *all* up in your stuff today," and the Boyfriend really was: I felt like I was somewhat unwillingly on a mini-retreat on trans-forming shame into medicine. It was amazing in a number of ways, and about time. I wore a loose red rubber band on my wrist to snap my way out of oc-casional non-forgiveness and I moved on.

Several months passed, during which I came upon the first letter of John, in which he writes, to paraphrase: reach out to people and don't be a jerk. This is something I will definitely whisper to my grandson from the great beyond. And it gave me a great idea: I would host an online fundraiser for a law firm in Berkeley that does pro bono work with LGBTQ refugees. The weakest of the weak, the Sermon on the Mount writ large and local. You want to feel the physical, vibrational presence of Jesus on this side of things? Go sit in the waiting room someplace where public servants are tending to the most marginalized in our society.

In general, if I announce I have a good idea for you, back away slowly. Then run. But this time I was sure. What could possibly go wrong?

I knew the head of this law firm, the forty-year-old daughter of lifelong friends and an absolutely superior human being. Here was this woman doing fabulous work on so many levels. I could pull in money for her, and doing it might balance things out, or even tip me out of the red.

She was excited by my offer, and a committee began spreading the word far and wide of a fund-raiser featuring girl writer Anne Lamott. Then I made the cardinal sin of being too pleased with myself. Two days later, *ring ring ring*. It was my friend's daughter, and she sounded worried. She said that one of her board members had heard that I was transphobic. She said how embarrassed she was but that the board member needed assurance from me that I had changed.

In the glacial pause that followed, I had what felt like either an MSG attack or a stroke. There I was on the blacktop again being bullied as a child, proving once again that Faulkner was right: "The past is never dead. It's not even past." There I was in high school while my beloved teacher read to the class the paragraphs in the essay on *Moby-Dick* that I'd plagiarized from CliffsNotes, and then the

CliffsNotes. And there I was in the lifelong nightmare of appearing onstage in my underpants.

The best I could do in the moment was to splut-
ter that I never had been transphobic. I had done a
stupid, hurtful thing and everything I could since
to counterbalance it.

There was another long sheet-metal pause.

She said, and I quote, "Well, she wants to know
that you've evolved."

This was a showstopper. And it's what finally
helped me break through.

I said I had always been like this, centered
in my values of loving and affirming the LGBTQ
community.

She was embarrassed and apologetic but said,
"Could you just give her some reassurance, something easy for her to gulp down?" Like perhaps a
raspberry smoothie?

I reminded myself: reach out to people and
don't be a jerk—and also, if possible, breathe. Somehow I managed all three.

"Look," I said, "I cannot do this with you. Give
her my last book, where there's an essay on this experience, on contrition and grace. Give her all my
work over the last forty years. This is who I am. I
cannot have these discussions anymore. It saps me.
It makes me so sad."

I was teary. I think she was, too. There were more long silences until I said: "I'll do whatever you and the board want. I'm glad to step aside and use my social media to drum up business for a replacement. I'll make a donation. Anything for the fundraiser to go well. I love you, honey, but don't talk to me about evolution. I am where I am. I know who I am. We'll talk soon."

I was mortified that she would talk about this with her parents and their illustrious and spiritually savvy friends, and they would all be shocked. Down inside the old wound, the infection whispered that I'd done something repellent, because I am a repellent person. The shame felt almost like a fever. But I had said that I know who I am and so I set about catching up to that.

Who am I? Pretty much the same as you. Human, flawed, gorgeous.

I put the law firm's name in the God box and prayed, "Here, O Israel, or Jesus, Mary—Whoever happens to be on call right now. Help." An anonymous rabbi once said, "Jesus was a great prophet with a lot of great ideas," and then added, "some of them new." I love this, and love the Hebrew Bible. I read psalms to my Sunday school kids about the goodness of God, who is so weirdly merciful and compassionate, slow to anger, and always ready to forgive, no matter what we have done. (You have to ask yourself, what's the catch?) The kids feel ashamed when they miss the target, are mean to each other, to other kids, and to their parents. To-gether, we speak to God in silence with our eyes closed and say we are sorry, and after a while we open our eyes and I assure them that they are now forgiven. Then we have snacks and get out the box of art supplies. It's a great system.

I told Neal and Sam what had happened with the law firm fundraiser, and they were furious on my behalf. It felt good that they had my back, but there I was dangling in limbo. A girl has to wonder if it is worth it at this late age, with this thin skin, to be in the public eye.

Then apricity kicked in, urging me to turn to what comforted me and to the outpouring of sup-port that I was getting from those who love me, those who know I am not transphobic, and good old Mother Nature snorfling my neck. Somehow, at some point, the fever broke and I was regular old flawed human me again.

I didn't hear back right away, but I was done with explaining myself, equally ready to go ahead with the fundraiser and ready to step aside. The board could do what the board was going to do, and it had nothing to do with who I am. The world is not fair and rarely forgiving, and I still get furious and saddened about that. My only option at this point was to choose radical self-love—a bath, lots of lotion, a cup of tea, and the latest issue of *People* magazine as the day's scripture. I felt more or less safe. The longest twenty inches on Earth are from the brain to the heart.

The minute I say to the shame, "Oh, you again," I've won. The wicked witch melts into a pool until the next time. I am not who I am when I screw up, but also, I suppose, the dean is not who she was when she sent out that letter, nor the board member asking if I had evolved.

As it turns out, the board came crawling back, as I'd hoped it would, inviting me enthusiastically to participate. I gave a fabulous talk, and the law firm made a ton of money for this amazing organization. The team sent me the lushest, most beautiful bouquet the next day with, as God is my witness, coin-shaped eucalyptus leaves on stalks amid the roses. Eucalyptus leaves always smell woodsy, minty, fresh. You had to laugh.

The florist left the bouquet in a vase sitting on a bench in the sun on the front porch. The eucalyptus is my tree, like pelicans are my bird and daisies are my flower. Any eucalyptus grove has something ecclesiastical about it because each tree gives off a silvery glow. The endlessly tall trunks are so erect and organized, almost harmonious, with lush leaves all the way up to the Dr. Seuss top-knots. There is an orderly and uplifted feeling in a grove, like in a cathedral's architecture and light. Houses of worship are supposed to somehow bring both peace and vitality into your body and soul, and somehow those trees do that too when I manage to be quiet and still in their presence. On the bench on our porch, the round silvery-green leaves in the vase looked wet with sunlight.

SIX

Song

Twenty years ago I first came across the Indian writer Arundhati Roy's beautiful statement "Another world is not only possible, she is on her way. On a quiet day, I can hear her breathing." I scribbled it down and taped it to my computer. I have taped it to every computer I have had since, to remind me that if I stop to listen, I will hear hope. I hear it in nature, in singing, in stories of goodness, in the saddest places, in celebration, but maybe most often in gently absurd stories of love.

On a weekend not long ago when family and political messes had me down, a friend happened to call. He told me about a friend of his named Paul who took in a family of Ukrainian refugees. Paul and his wife had a small guesthouse in their back-yard with two little bedrooms. Their grown son had come to them and said, "The refugee organi-zation in town is looking for people to take in a family. We should do this." Paul and his wife said to each other, "He's right. It's a good thing that our son wants this, and we should respond to his gen-erosity. We should live up to who he thinks we are." The wife is an expert in eastern European music and had once directed a choir that sang sacred songs from Ukraine, Georgia, and Russia. With a little imagination, it seemed a good fit.

One night a translator arrived with a shell-shocked family of four—husband, wife, teenager, and eight-year-old. None of them spoke English. Paul and his family pantomimed welcome and gladness. The first night, because of a plumbing problem in the guesthouse, they had to stay inside Paul's house, the parents in the guest room and the two boys in the bedrooms of their sons.

The next day, Paul took the family out to the guesthouse. He showed them how all the various systems worked, and they listened attentively, but when he went to leave, they followed him back to the main house like ducklings.

They were tired, sad, and hurting, and they

didn't want to be alone, so Paul let them stay in the main house the first week.

The couple was in the guest room next door to Paul and his wife's, and through the walls he heard them whispering urgently in Ukrainian late into the night. Paul would ask the translator to come by and explain that the guesthouse was all theirs, so both families could have privacy. But the translator responded apologetically that the Ukrainian couple was too afraid to stay in the little house with their sad lonely feelings and devastating memories of war. The translator told them, "They don't want to be alone. They want to be with you."

Paul hadn't bargained for or agreed to this much love and mercy, and as the days passed, he was both irritated and deeply moved by this family's honest need. And so he let them stay in the (not very big) main house for a while longer.

One day Paul emailed my friend and said: "I want to move out. I'm like, take my house. I'll take the guesthouse." But he also told my friend that the two families cooked together, that the eight-year-old was enrolled in school and was picking up English quickly, and that the two families now shared a life together. The children went to school while the parents largely kept to themselves in the guest room until it was time to help with dinner.

My friend wrote back that resistance was futile, that love makes you soft if you are not careful, and that he was sorry but it was clearly too late for Paul.

There were six Ukrainian families in Paul's town, and the refugee organization brought over another family that spoke English so they could translate for the other. And it turned out that the family had understood all along what Paul was trying to tell them, about moving to their own house, but they didn't want to do that. They said, "Ask if it would be okay if we stayed with them a little bit longer. We'll go out there if they *want* us to, but we really like staying with them."

Paul felt their need, their vulnerability, how deeply traumatized these strong Ukrainian people were, so of course they could stay in the house with Paul and his wife.

Paul had had sons, so he knew some of the things boys love, and so he started wrestling with the little boy. They built a sweet bond, but still Paul dreaded coming home some nights. He said the days were both racing by and moving like syrup. Then one morning Paul's wife sang a Ukrainian song from her old eastern European choir days while making breakfast, and the other woman joined in. It turned out that she knew the songs the wife could sing in Ukrainian. Together the sound was quite beautiful. Still, Paul prayed directly to them: "Please move into the guesthouse. We will not abandon you. We'll eat lots of meals together. I'm such a good guy for bringing you here to live with us. And I'll bring you some nice food in the morning. That's a lot!" He would wake up just wanting to have coffee and read the paper in peace and quiet, but the little boy would want to practice his English with Paul and the Ukrainian father would have peevish rapid-fire conversations with his teenage son, and it would all seem hopeless. And then the wives would begin to sing.

Love is how hope takes flight, in swamps and barren fields, arising in different frequencies, blending the way sound vibrations of different pitches organize to make music. With my failing hearing in our failing world, I try to listen for this song underneath the river of incoming data and my pinball machine mind and I find that it is always playing.

I was taking the slowest walk humanly possible one day with a sad, scared friend who had been diagnosed out of the blue with a fatal disease. She had just thought she might be anemic. She has competed in two triathlons, and now a two-mile walk took us two and a half hours. It is not fair. Fair is where the pony rides are. Decades ago I ran (slowly) with her on mountain trails and when I had to stop because of my aging feet, we'd walk until my feet felt better. I can show you dozens of places I've walked with her: the salmon-spawning spots, the route past the stables, or the highest trails from which you can almost see Tokyo: once when we arrived at the top, with her sprinting and me behind her, doubled over gasping for breath, we spotted a tennis ball wedged into a huge sprawling oak, in the crook of a branch five feet off the ground. We thought it must be a tennis ball tree, bearing the first fruit of the season. The tree is so ancient that some of its branches reach out for twenty feet and then bend down to touch the ground.

Was that first sighting of the tree really twenty years ago? I have no idea. It could be ten. She couldn't remember either. Time is a complete mystery to me, and I'm not sure anyone really knows what time is. Douglas Adams wrote, "Time is an illusion. Lunchtime doubly so." But it *was* lunchtime, and I had brought us a lunch of cheese and avocado sandwiches, her favorite, mayonnaise being the main ingredient.

After lunch we hobbled on like ancient monks out for a walk at the Old Monks' Home. "This walk is making me *gain* weight," I complained. We ended up in a grove of redwoods where sky peeked through the canopy of trees like blue jigsaw pieces. Life is such a mystery that you have to wonder if God drinks a little. How did my youngish, athletic friend get this disease? It must have been on a day when God was drinking tequila.

My friend filled me in on all the latest lab work and then said, "Please tell me how you are and what you know. If you can make me laugh, I will pay you."

"How much?"

I told her about the Ukrainian refugees. She clutched her heart. "I love it." She looked at me gently. "I'm your Ukrainian refugee now."

"We're all each other's Ukrainian refugees."

We stopped to listen to the silence. Then she passed gas as loudly as a tuba. We howled with laughter and for the rest of the walk kept giggling off and on. We felt lifted on an updraft, lighter and silly, which can be a rare occurrence if you don't know whether you are going to live a few months or a year. As if any of us do.

That we all have an unknown expiration date was the message of Yom Kippur later in the week. I celebrated at sunset with hundreds of people from Temple Emanu-El, where my wild and brilliant friend Syd Mintz is a rabbi. She had lured me into her web a few days earlier on her houseboat in Sausalito, where she lives with her wife. She is ten years younger than I, small, with dark boy-cut hair and horn rims, clear-eyed and animated.

I told her, "My friend Teri Goodman was mistaken for you at a wedding recently, so she blessed everyone."

"Thank her for me."

I had explained to Syd that I really couldn't do the Yom Kippur ceremony for many excellent reasons, mostly having to do with how I hate to leave my house at all, and that I actively dread small talk with strangers, which normal people seem not to mind. I find it stultifying and it strips me of all hope. But I agreed to hear her out.

To begin, she went out on the deck and blew a shofar, a ram's-horn trumpet, the voice of heaven, rich and sacred. Because I am a Philistine, I had to stifle giggles because I instantly thought of my gassy friend in the redwood grove.

She said, "It's an incredibly powerful celebration, the day of facing our own mortality. Once a year we face ourselves, we face God, and we face one another with our souls totally bared in sacred song, and I promise, it is a joyous event. We throw breadcrumbs in the water to symbolize what we are willing to hand over to God. It's kind of a

preamble to death as a path to becoming fully
alive. I don't know if the end is tomorrow or if
I'm going to live to be ninety. So how do I live in
the face of that? Maybe kinder, less greedy, more
prayerful? Maybe I have more fun?"

That actually didn't sound awful. "When my
dad got sick," I said, "he said that we were all on
borrowed time, and it was good to be reminded of
this now and then. But I'm grieving for a friend
who out of the blue learned that she may die rather
soon or not for a while, and who simply does not
know."

"Neither do you or I," Syd pointed out. "You
know the Leonard Cohen song 'Who by Fire'? 'Who
shall I say is calling?' Cancer? Fire? Age?"

"To me," I said, "that is profound, but not exactly joyous."

"Trust me. Sunset, with several hundred Jews
singing, at Baker Beach."

"That's a lot of Jews," I said.

"You're telling *me*."

I got up to leave for my church, a five-minute
drive away. "Think about it," she said. "About
whether you might leave behind your critical voice,
your greed and people-pleasing patterns. Or at
least let them be weakened."

"You will have to pry them from my cold dead

hands," I interrupted. "You do your little pitch, Syd, and I'll do mine at the other end of the beach: 'Try harder at everything. Hoard. Amass. Cling to self-promotion and perfectionism.' I'll tell them it's why people respect you."

"I'll send you instructions."

She emailed me some descriptions of Yom Kippur, the Day of Atonement, the end of the ten days that begin with Rosh Hashanah, the New Year. I was to ask myself in the coming days: What could I leave behind in the surf? And especially, what kind of life did I want to return to?

I tried to imagine being at the edge of the ocean, throwing breadcrumbs into the surf along with millions of people all over the world, who were each opening up their hearts, bravely casting their shortcomings and disappointments into the ocean as one, and it made me tense as a terrier. What if strangers tried to talk to me? Or, by the same token, what if it worked and I returned home lighter, more *here* for this one short life? Or . . . what if it worked for everyone there but me, and I skulked off the beach at the end of the service as narcissistic and people-pleasing as ever? And everyone could see that I was a hopeless case, and they recoiled, pulling their children to safety behind them?

In the end I found myself in the car on Yom Kippur, driving to Baker Beach.

As I drove through the Presidio, I thought about what I might leave in the surf, and after a bit I imagined a showroom to which I brought you if I needed you to love and respect me. I showed you the fine, polished car of me that you eventually purchased. The car was freshly painted so you wouldn't notice all its problems, but not too long after driving it off the lot you would realize that it was a lemon. The engine rattled, the gas tank leaked, the upholstery seams were splitting. But I had let you fall in love with its sleek curves and sound system.

I wanted to give up the fear that you fell in love with the car of me in the showroom only to find out that the brakes were worn and a spring was coming through the upholstery, that I'd tricked you into wanting me but now you were stuck.

I wanted to come back to a purer place in myself for which I don't have words.

There were four or five hundred people on the beach, under a sky awash in rose and orange tones, with flecks of gold glitter like eternity must look: Turkish playwright Mehmet Murat İldan wrote, "Sunset is the opening music of the night." Families were gathered in front of the stage, where Syd, the cantor, a choir, and some musicians were banging out a sacred song in Hebrew. On blankets and on the sand, stretching back forever, they stood in small groups talking, singing, laughing, and running along the tide with their kids and dogs. I stopped in the middle of the crowd and sang along with the next song, "Rivers of Babylon." When Syd saw me, her mouth dropped open, and she leapt down from the stage to hug me. Did you see that, everybody, how I'm the teacher's pet? She took me to a blanket where her elderly mother and grown son sat with their posses, and I was enveloped in warmth. She went on to mingle with other congregants, and the musicians onstage sang favorite songs of mine, "Bridge over Troubled Water" and "Down to the River to Pray." I got up because I wanted to dance and sing, but when I stood up I felt shy for a moment, with hunched shoulders like a vulture or Richard Nixon. Then I began to sway.

The easiest way to get present is to sing, because you can't move to the next note until you've finished the one you're singing. So I sang with everything I had.

There were songs in Hebrew over the roar of the surf and the multitudes, and then Syd took the stage again. She announced that for environmental reasons, we would not be throwing breadcrumbs into the water after all, but rather we would write in the sand what we wanted to leave for God. She said, "Write down what you're sick of carrying, all the stuff that you lug around because you have all the time in the world. Yom Kippur says you don't. Leave here what you can. Leave your jealousy, your self-scrutiny, your obsession with wealth, your weight, your stature, yourself."

We went in disorganized shifts to the edge of the ocean, and people drew a word or two in the sand with their forefingers, for the tide to sweep back into the sea. I drew a primitive sports car. The band kept playing, Hebrew songs, "Dock of the Bay," and then, magically, my favorite song of the past fifty years, "Ripple" by the Grateful Dead. (It can't really have been fifty years, can it?) Neal and I discovered on our second date that it was the song we both wanted played at our memorial services. We chose it for my wedding processional, and the late great Jerry Garcia sang as if he were still alive— because he is—as I walked down the aisle in a redwood grove on my younger brother's arm. I sang it now with hundreds of people surrounding me. I felt like a tuning fork. I remembered once seeing a film of deaf kids listening to a piano in class through their fingertips, with their whole bodies hearing the music through their tummies and their hands and the oneness of the experience. I sang and heard the others singing "Ripple" through the very heart of me, connecting with each other and me. I felt very exposed and a little unhinged, and it was good.

I had so much residual warmth on the drive home that I didn't even put on the radio. Warmth is love in its plainest clothing. When I got to our house, I found Neal reading on the couch with the dogs. I gave him a detailed report, ending with the serendipity that the last song they played before the closing Hebrew hymn was "Ripple."

"No way."

"Way." He was happy hearing this and gave me a thumbs-up. That we found each other in the swirl and chaos can still make me shake my head with gratitude and relief. He bought the showroom car of me and loves it even more for all its dents and worrisome sounds. What were the odds of the two of us finding each other so late in life, still young enough to do it all? Maybe it has worked in the long term because we stayed in the soda shop stage for so long early on, talking away in coffeehouses, hiking, watching TV. On our tenth date, though, which was ten days after our first meeting,

Somehow

Neal and I were sitting across from each other at a small table in our favorite café in the county, and I made a move, hussy that I am. I reached past the sugar and the salt, touched the tip of his forefinger with mine, and rubbed his fingernail. Maybe it was not the ceiling of the Sistine Chapel, but deep inside I felt a reverberation, vibrations of joy and fear, the sound of a whole new world on its way.

SEVEN

Cowboy

If you ever find yourself all turned around underwater and can't tell which way is up, blow bubbles and swim in their direction to the surface. Odds are that people will be waiting up above who were worried when you dropped out of sight. They've been trying to bail out the ocean, frantic to find you. They will cry with relief, just as you would have if one of them had gone under. Community is a body of people crying for one another, working together for a common cause, enjoying and overlooking (or grimly tolerating) each other's foibles; it's a rough and beautiful quilt sewn of patches that don't seem to go together at all, and then do.

Community means we're collaborating. It means that you help my children and my old people and I help yours. It means we are in this together. Most of us are perhaps a tiny bit self-absorbed, and good at keeping out people who don't look, vote, or act like our friends, and that's very nice. But a good community includes all those other people and those of us at the edges. Welcomes are offered: hey, come on into the circle—yeah, you. You with your nose in the air, or a neck tattoo, a walker or a Rolls.

Through an unknowable force, people join together to fight for what they think is right, or to bird-watch, or feed the poor, to help one another stay sober or rebuild after natural catastrophes. There are crazy communities—"We're going to be raptured and F you and isn't God great"—and groups of volunteer do-gooders who are the main reason anything works at all.

Odd, anxious people like me come together and then stick around awhile. It is uncomfortable and metamorphic; nobody in isolation becomes who they were designed to be.

Frederick Buechner wrote: "You can survive on your own. You can grow strong on your own. You can even prevail on your own. But you cannot become human on your own." This is unfortunate. I think Jesus would agree that some people are incredibly annoying. (Many days He had to lie down with a cold compress on his head.)

Years ago my great friend Mark Yaconelli had a wonderful pastor at his small progressive church: humble, loving, and real. She put a notice in the church newsletter letter one week saying: "I'm starting a radical Jesus group. If you are interested, show up Tuesday night at seven o'clock." Twenty people showed up the first night. She had them sit in a circle and announced that she wanted to follow the radical Jesus, He of service and reckless love, and she was going to need others to do this with her. She didn't quite know what that might look like, though, so she threw it out there. A few people said they needed to start a homeless shelter in the church, build showers and serve meals. Someone else said that the local radio station was run by a right-wing media company, putting out hate, and they should arrange a boycott of this station, or drown out its voice of hate with community concerts and a joyful boisterous Pride parade. They could convert the church to solar power. Everybody had great ideas of how they could share the goodness of God, and be better stewards of our poor Earth. But when they were done, the pastor said, "This is all good stuff, but I feel exhausted. Your ideas seem to spring from anger and despair. I don't know how we're going to do all this. Why doesn't everybody go pray about it and come back next week?"

Most people came back the following week, except this time people were prepared, which meant they had arguments for why the group should or shouldn't do whatever, whether it was to create a homeless shelter, drown out right-wing radio, or save the planet. The emotional environment in the room was resentment and competitive distress. People were trying to convert each other to how a community should be run, and who—hint, hint— should run it.

At the end of *this* meeting, the pastor said: "I'm already regretting starting this radical Jesus group. You're so unhappy with each other. I don't know what to do."

Then someone suggested, "Maybe we should be radical Jesus to each other before we go out and help the world." And the pastor jumped on that. She asked everyone to go home that week and ask in prayer what each of them needed, and how the radical Jesus of crazy compassion could help them. The following week, they would come with one way they would like to be helped, and then maybe they could learn something from that.

Only ten came back the next week. One woman said she struggled with her weight and tried many diets but none was working. She thought if she could take a walk every morning, she would feel better and asked if anyone would be willing to take a walk with her. Two women raised their hands. Another woman said she loved to host people for dinner but a year earlier had hosted a couple and not remembered their dietary needs—one was vegan, one was gluten-free. She had been afraid and ashamed to have anyone over since then. Would someone be willing to come over to her house for dinner? All of the people raised their hands.

One man said his dad had been a handyman who could fix anything in the house but never showed him how to do anything. He had a bath-room sink that had been broken for about two months and was too ashamed to call anybody be-cause his handyman father would never allow his wife to call a repairman. Could someone come and help him fix his sink? Somebody raised a hand. Everyone shared what made them feel vulnerable, and everyone allowed others to help them.

My friend Mark's request was a feeling of

spinning out all the time with workaholism and obsessive distractions, and he needed someone to sit and pray with him. He wouldn't do it unless another person sat with him in the silence and just let God love him. It was the pastor who volunteered for that one. She would go to his house and sit with Mark in silence. She'd call first to set it up and he'd say, "Well, I got a lot going on—deadlines, etc. I can't do it today." And she would say, "Mark, you asked me to hold you accountable, so I'm going to come over to your house anyway and I'll just sit on your porch." He'd say, "Shit." But he'd meet her on the porch. And it was gorgeous. They cried together sometimes. They laughed a lot. They sat in silence.

And after the people in the group had been caring for one another for a while, the original dreams came true: they remodeled the church basement to make showers for the homeless, started a soup kitchen, went solar, and helped start a Pride parade for the town.

Funny how this love business works.

One of my communities includes eight women in their seventies and eighties; we've been together for ten years. I asked them to be bridesmaids at my wedding, which took place in a redwood grove a five-minute walk from my house. I have luscious younger girlfriends I could have asked to do the honors (well, one). The eight of us originally met in a gathering of people trying to heal from tiny control issues, many of whom, like me, had kids who were addicts who had had kids. Having tried unsuccessfully to save, fix, and rescue our children, we had set upon theirs, our precious grandchildren. Some of our hostages were babies and toddlers, some older, but we were all fixated on saving them from their parents, and we were going nuts. We met up when the meeting was over and agreed to reconvene soon. We fished each other out of the delusion that our children should listen to our good idea, and that our help was helpful. We have been meeting every two weeks ever since for ten years. As we got well, our kids got well. Even today, we listen, groan, laugh, and smite our foreheads at our crazy controlling schemes. Horribly, our kids still do not seem to want our help and excellent advice. We frequently have to remind each of the acronym WAIT—Why am I talking? When we don't interfere, the kids like and love us, and we are now able to accept them pretty much as is, and love them unconditionally (most of the time), depending on how we've slept.

In the wake of the Umpqua Community College shootings in Oregon, where nine people died and nine were wounded, a man who installed cable made a sign out of metal. He fashioned it into the shape of Oregon, and cut out a little heart for the town of Roseburg, where the shooting happened. He put it on Facebook and said, "I'm selling these for fifty bucks. I'm going to give all the money to the victims." And in the aftermath of grief and hopelessness, he started getting hundreds and hundreds of offers. So he put out word to the town that he needed help to cut the metal and the hearts, and paint them, and collect the money, and set up a website so people could see that the group was not a grift. He started getting 150 people a night showing up at his house. This lasted for two months. He had to set up porta-potties outside his house to deal with the volunteers. Someone was in charge of feeding everyone, someone was in charge of the paints, others for the shipping and the bookkeeping. The group fulfilled all the orders in about two months, but people kept coming over to have that experience. This is what matters most, being together in spirit, helping and letting people help us. We are a complicated species, and keeping things simple when possible seems to work best for us.

Whales are complex creatures, too, and a lot like us in the sense that many of them have very close familial bonds. For orcas, family connections are quite strong, and we know they pitch in to help care for other members of their family, share the prey that they catch, and help babysit younger members in the group if Mom is busy. There was a Bigg's orca in the Salish Sea known as T2C2, or "Tumbo." He had scoliosis and would often lag behind his family. He wasn't able to take part in hunts like the rest of the group, but for more than a decade other whales slowed down and made sure to feed him.

In the recovery community we say, "The opposite of addiction is not sobriety, it's connection." Some people find true connection at work, in motorcycle gangs, mosques or churches or synagogues or yoga studios. Some people have found it working in soup kitchens, at town cleanups, mentoring, with mountain bikers. People like me, left to my own devices, keep judging who is or isn't fine enough to audition for our herds. I find this instinct repellent when I see it in others. It keeps me separate from you, from me, from life.

I found my way into two seriously spooky groups when I hit bottom: I joined my church drunk, and a year later I got suckered into trying to stay sober for just one day, thirty-seven years ago. I'd always loved being alone and still do. I used to feel there was something mythic in being insulated, fending off life's dangers alone, the hero in a Jack London story, by myself in the woods with only a fire and courage, the eyes of wolves glinting upon me. The lone wolf watching it all from a distance is such a romantic image, but he is actually the most vulnerable in the pack. Isolating from the herd does not keep you safe, except from disease. The isolating instinct is what mortally injured animals do, those who don't want to be a burden on the group. But hardly anyone would be a burden to any of the groups I belong to. In community, lines of difference blur. We get hydrated, and we get our senses of humor back, the great miracle; we get set back on our feet when we fall or get knocked down, and we're filled up by helping other people get back on their feet. My friend Father Terry Richie said, "The gift is that you get to rejoice in watching someone else get well." The gift is caring.

You don't have to get it together to find a community; in fact, you might not be able to get it together until you join. You're a human being and that's enough. We're damaged and beautiful, egocentric, loving, driven or not driven enough, and we all have work to contribute. We all have a lot to learn, as individuals and as a body. Solitude is one kind of classroom, while communities transmit intergenerational knowledge. The elders teach us how to be patient and the kids teach us how to stay young.

In most of my communities, I've arrived toxic or banged up by life, and strangers showed me how to get back on track. When you've run out of any more good ideas and voice (even silently) that you need help, the next thing you know you'll be directed to people who are sorting used clothes for Africa, or in sanghas meditating or in basements staying sober or square dancing in a nearby field every Saturday. They have found connection with other human beings. Eighty percent of any meeting or gathering might be stupid and beneath you, but the other twenty percent will save you: it will open up your brain and expand your life and give you connection, a place in the family of man. And this is salvation.

They will offer you the sacrament of welcome. But to keep it, you must give it away. Giving and receiving is the economy of our souls. This will fill you, and if you are not careful it will radicalize you. What certain kinds of parents told us about who we were was actually about who *they* were, while a friendly community holds up a more accurate mirror, revealing that there are others in the frame. No matter how hard I try, I cannot sing harmony by myself. We are part of something that is kind of magical. Come take your place at the table. The throne is the loneliest seat in the house. Sometimes tribes are thriving, sometimes they are hurting. It is how life works. We thrive, we hide behind our masks, we take risks, our lives get bigger. We fall apart, we rebuild; life, death, new life.

As a skinny teenager and an only child, my son found that Emerson's essay on self-reliance—this idea that you could build yourself up, create a completely self-sustaining person, and find freedom in not needing anyone—spoke to him. And while he now teaches kids self-reliance in the outdoors, he also helps them bond. His community of tree-hugging kids is learning independence, autonomy, and survival, and there's a beauty to that, and there's beauty in how they look out for each other. My son also belongs to a group of sober men who share a mission to be good men, partners, and parents. They drink coffee and tell each other the truth about their appalling setbacks and small victories, and in so doing, unhook from their own monkey minds, and in listening and caring, hook into something much bigger. This is freedom.

How to find a beloved community? You just have to want to. Then you wander shyly into some group or other that has caught your eye, that you've heard or read about—the local birders, parents with special-needs children, the marijuana addicts. You show up, you step inside. Maybe like me you feel like a walking personality disorder but manage to say hello. A lot of things start with hello. Maybe someone offers you a glass of water. You say, "Thank you." You drink it, and then you look back at them and you say, "Could you tell me a little about what all of you are up to here?" I honestly think you can do this. If I could—introverted, narcissistic me—you can.

Becoming part of a community can be scary initially, even if you have been feeling lonely and untethered. We worry we will get lost or used or taken advantage of or mocked, or we'll disappear, or we'll get equalized, so that a lifetime of high achievement, of being a very special person in the world, will have been for naught.

The hard part is coming a second time. Maybe you're not convinced that these people are worthy of you or think that they would never accept you. But almost always people will say, "We're glad to see you. Please come back." And you'll think, well, they're just nuts. Or they're a cult, and they'll make me sleep with the leader, or get a tattoo in a very special place. But they'll just say, "We're glad to see you." You think that, sadly, you don't have time for this because you're a busy and important person.

Then if you do come back three or four times because you have the gift of desperation, you'll see
someone come in who's clearly there for the first
time, looking furtive, arrogant, or shy. So *you* go
up to them and you say, "Hello. I'm glad you're
here."

Of course, there are also cults of bizarre religious folks, initially beatifically welcoming, and
armed ones whose mission is to control, overthrow,
or prosper, often in the name of God—in fact,
almost always in the name of God. Poor God. If
someone wants your money or unquestioning alle-
giance, run. If they don't agree with you about who
the president is, back away slowly. If they seem to
have good hearts and their purpose interests or
excites you, I would listen to that. As Mel Brooks
said, "Listen to your broccoli and your broccoli
will tell you how to eat it." You'll just know.

Whole towns in California were devastated by
fires a couple of years ago. People showed up and
spontaneously said things like, "The traffic lights
are out, I'll station myself at this intersection all
day long and help direct traffic." Nobody asked
them to do it. It was this lovely thing where people
were directing traffic all over the city. That goodness is the true self showing up. That goodness of
working together toward the common good is the

most powerful force on Earth. And that goodness leads to hope. People told strangers they didn't have a way to get back to where their houses and cars had been, and strangers said, "Take my car. You need a car—go." Towns put together bike brigades because people were stuck in homes with no water or electricity, but couldn't leave because streets were blocked with debris and burnt-out vehicles. So a call went out to anybody with a bicycle. "Come help; either ride a bike to haul water in these backpacks or loan a bike to somebody who can." Thousands of people showed up across the state during our worst fires with bikes and maps, figuring out how to get to someone who might be cut off, and how to bring them water, a little medical aid, some food and love.

That's not charity. It is the reality of being human, of needing help and being helpers. This is who we are, this is our true selves. We have been the person trapped and the person biking to them. Love is call-and-response.

There is a flow among people gathered together for the common good, the flow of intuitively sensing who needs what, and it's a rare and exquisite flow. In basketball they call this full-court vision, where players know where their teammates are without looking. They know that so-and-so is running up the righthand side toward the basket, and they pass the ball behind their back to him or her. You saw Magic Johnson do this all the time: throw the ball over his head behind him, not even looking, just knowing his guy was coming. You see that kind of flow when people work together in food kitchens, in music and dance, where bodies express a reality in which the illusion of separateness disappears. We see and grok each other, intuit each other's humanity if even for a moment or two, and maybe in so doing see our own.

All over our county I've watched and helped playgrounds rise in poorer areas, women and men working all day to build them, because the local kids were hurting, desperately needing space to play. You saw people sweating, sawing, nailing, laughing, groaning at the weight of the wood or steel, others bringing the workers sandwiches, cookies, coffee. It was paradise. It washed away judgment, sarcasm, hierarchies, and, best of all, the fixation with oneself and one's appearance. It was grassroots magic—as most magic is. It was also usually the best thing I'd done in any given year.

Beyond the disguises, personas, and masks, we are also animals, and communities of animals are fascinating. When other animals venture out of the woods, we tap our companion on the shoulder and say, "God, look at those elk!" Watching salmon spawn, we're instantly in awe. We are too used to ourselves to notice what amazing creations we are, and not just babies and pro athletes. Regular people serving and being served in soup kitchens, people who line up to vote when you are working the polls, let alone all the other poll workers. People cleaning up beaches and trails.

Intimate groups take longer to form, but we are doomed without them. Our lives stay small, although we get to keep thinking in our isolation that we are right. Communities are where the spirit does the deep work of evolution, away from small and superior, to deeper and messier and more alive. Even though I won't go to parties and risk being taken hostage to small talk, I host holiday gatherings three times a year, family and a motley crew of old friends and stragglers. My way at a group meal is to hang back and either ask questions, or tell stories, or show off knowledge. I'm always secretly wondering, "Are you on or am I on? Who's got the microphone?" But the love of that group is that they see me, the false parts of myself that I'm propping up, and they say, "Okay, you need to do that." It's like seeing a kid who needs to dress in a cowboy outfit for dinner every night: Okay, that's what you need to do. You're not really a cowboy, but if you want to dress up like that for dinner, that's fine with us. And you want us to call you Carl. We're glad to. But we love you so much anyway and your dressing up is not the thing we love about you.

And Carl R Us. Or at least Carl R Me.

To feel seen and known that way is holy; it's almost certainly been a long time coming. Love among others is the ocean, with tides, krill, and weird, beautiful fish, and love is a pond or a pool where we teach little kids to swim—first showing them that something holds them up in the water, then how to blow bubbles on the surface, and then how to blow bubbles underwater, so they can always find their way back up.

EIGHT

Up Above

If there is a hell, besides the ones we have all known on Earth, it will not include eternal flames and your wife's sister but will be an attic with just enough light so you can make out the eyes of the rats in the dark. They will look up from eating some stuff that we don't even consider edible, such as the glue that binds one's favorite college textbooks, and anything else they can get their pointy yellow teeth into. In hell, they will wink at you and make the sign of a chef's kiss, then scuttle away into the shadows. They will come back later to eat a hole through your boxes of papers and mementos, which would be tragic if the suspicion didn't arise later in life that these treasured objects are about as meaningful as participation medals from swim class for putting your head underwater. The rats will line their nests with the writing award you won in junior high, vacation photos with former friends dating back to the Carter administration, and the newspaper clipping from *The Modesto Bee* sixty years ago that mentions you had advanced to the semifinals of the twelve-and-under tennis championship, a clipping that has been moved in the same box a dozen times and that the rats have turned into a pretty attractive doily.

Does this buffet of your achievements start to argue for the absurdity of life? Well, yes and no. Life can be absurd, sure, but also full of such touching courage—not that of the resistance fighter but of a simple human being who bravely tried hard things and bore the withering losses of life and family, who dared to let people know them and love them.

Under these peaked attic ceilings, on millions of streets, are shabby museums that preserve our tokens of love and loss, our joys, pretensions, catastrophes, and resurrections, the whole holy enchilada. The party favors, souvenirs, and awards are the merch from life's bewildering gift shop. And several years ago I moved all of mine again to begin a new life with the man I would marry, and his boxes.

My most fertile attic was five houses away from where we live now, where my grandchild Jax came to life, where Sam bottomed out, where Neal and I fell in love. The mementos that collected in that attic for my ten years there were squares along the Chutes and Ladders path that led me to now. To Sam, who is a miracle. To marvelous teenage Jax. To lovely, steady Neal.

It was at that house where Neal and I had months of that oceanic feeling of new love, of knowing we wanted to keep the conversation going forever, like I have with a few lifelong friends. And then we learned to do ordinary life together with stomach flus, flooded basements, budgets, and our first small fights. These fights are not preserved with the travel photos and wedding paraphernalia, but the worst remain in the file cabinet of my mind.

There has been a basic format from the start: Every so often, Annie does not get her way, or Neal says something superior and provocative. Annie shuts down and becomes as quiet as the grave, while waiting for Neal to realize the gravity of his mistake and come crawling to her for forgiveness. (One can hope.) Annie and Neal sit together grimly on the couch ignoring each other while Annie thinks about how all men are pigs, until Neal leaps up to defend his position. Annie leaves the room, goes to the bedroom, and sulks. Neal barges in. Poor darling Annie is now crying. Neal stomps off, then comes back, having realized the gravity of his mistake and how completely doomed he is without her. Annie sits red-eyed, dangerous in a pathetic sort of way, the Hindu goddess Kali with PMS. Neal grows teary with love and contrition, which finally melts Annie's cold stone heart. It typically cycles through in an hour or so every few months.

Then we make up and start new conversations and create new memories and put photos of those in our boxes.

We started wanting to live together at some point, but the house was too small for the four of us, so we moved down the street with my son, grandson, a cat, the dogs, and our boxes. This meant spending a day in the old attic, poking through boxes, hopeful that I could get rid of a lot of stuff before we moved. Sam's fifth-grade report card, or mine? Nope. People frequently and annoyingly remind us that all we have is the eternal present, the holy moment, and to that I say, "Yeah, yeah, whatever," because in my boxes, I have Sam's and Jax's sonograms, my unfinished manuscripts, and my parents' death certificates. Still dead! Good to know. My mother saved every card my brothers and I ever made her. Life is not a tale told by an idiot: it's a mosaic made by elves on absinthe, of sunrises and vast starry nights, gluey gaps where tiles have fallen out; a copy of the ship's manifest from Ellis Island with my ten-year-old mother's and her twin sister's names, a photo of the indoor plant my dad gave me for my apartment when I first dropped out of college, very leafy and Rousseau. You could almost see a dinosaur under its fronds and you can see one now in the photo if you squint. Keepsakes from celebrations and a baggie of Sam's Scout badges, never sewn on, his achievements and my failures bound together for posterity.

Neal and I found a ramshackle compound down the street, a one-story Spanish Colonial in ruins set on rocky barren ground. There was a small barn in the back for Sam and Jax. We believed it could be beautiful, eventually. Meanwhile I was seated in the attic at home, bravely sorting through boxes I hadn't opened since the move *into* this house. Attics are so spooky, and I had to remind myself that courage is fear that has said its prayers.

The attic was the most fraught place of my childhood, full of menace. You knew that at any time all of it might drop down on you while you passed underneath, showering you with spiders and mice poo. In the attic of the house where Neal and I fell in love was a small window from which I occasionally saw the full moon above the magnolia. You can have the sun and its harsh glare, but leave me the moon. It softens the night. It is said that we bathe in moonlight, in its luminous bath, introspective, changeable, silver. It cools us; cools me down.

The window is the eye of the attic. What has it seen? What has it guarded?

The first thing that's tricky about attics is the ladder that unfolds out of the trapdoor. You tug down these rickety stairs, which gives you a shaky feeling already because stairs are not supposed to come from the ceiling except in Escher prints, and even then they're upside down. And when you pull down the attic hatch, the rope could break or become a noose—a thought common to children of alcoholics. But if you make it safely up the ladder, you've left reality, as if through a slightly uncomfortable portal, and you arise, waist high, like a swimmer, and look around. Often the light is almost imperceptible because there's a lot of dust, which makes it phantasmagorical, exactly what we've spent our lives trying to eradicate or deny:

life has way more layers and realities than we're comfortable with. This is the good news (again, eventually).

The bulb turns on reluctantly after tugging and tugging the long, frayed string.

As a child I obsessed about the madwoman I knew lived up in our attic. I know now she's us, the lowest, basest aspects of all humans. I never caught a glimpse of her, but sounds travel in the darkest night, so in bed in the dark I could hear her hawking and scratching. She considered my every move in her mad mind, eyes glinting. She was a witch—mean, bony, greedy, and judgmental, and when some nice person like me wanted or needed something, she wouldn't give it, and she gloated. She crouched over her resentments, like I do sometimes: they are her treasure.

It is not crazy to fear the attic. There are real and sometimes hairy spiders up there as well as depths of darkness in the corners, the scurrying of hidden vermin. And while you're being so brave up there, who knows what will happen down below? Someone could take the ladder away, or worse, raise it again and seal off the trapdoor with you inside. That was always the child's fear, abandonment. Every child knows why he or she should be exiled or caged: you are too annoying or needy, you're a scaredy-cat, an underperformer or a show-off, full of yourself. You can't deny what horrible times your parents went through when you were a child; such is life, and most children stood by helplessly, agreeing not to see. Likewise, denial doesn't work in the attic. You've entered, you've made the choice. You're there. You gaze at what you want to find and also what you don't want to see. But in order to find what you're looking for, you have to go through the boxed-up museum. It is the corn maze of the mind, where once you're in it, you're stuck and you have no idea how to get out. It's supposed to be fun, but it's tall stalks all around and you go around each corner and it's just more cornstalks and meanwhile your parents have gone off to have a drink or a fight.

Parents are constitutionally unable to throw out anything that their kids made. Almost all attics in America used to contain a clay ashtray with rounded indents where the child pressed her finger to create the place for the parent to rest their cigarette between sips. There are all the handprint turkeys from Thanksgivings, the books made of stapled index cards, the drawings, the report cards. Saving it all in a box meant you were a good parent. Your kids could find it if they ever wanted to, and their kids could sort through it for them someday. Wow, Mom had been really good at math! Who knew?

So that's all there in the banker's boxes at your feet, but what's also there are times that were sweet, fun, comically innocent, and even noble about your family's life—how touching were our efforts at courage and goodness, all mixed together. There were the common Raisin Bran moments of my own life that sustained me: long-term friendships, work, my brothers. And the vichyssoise experiences—in India, in love, in altered states, in concerts, in cathedrals—when I could merge briefly into the illimitable and be changed.

After my dad died, my younger brother and I brought Dad's boxes down from the attic and pawed through them, holding up things for each other to admire—*his* book reviews and mail. We tossed most of it. In one box, we found a nest of baby mice, blind and so helpless, and so like us. The mom must have gone to get food. We screamed and laughed, had another drink, and put the box out in the yard. Some animal probably ate them, maybe our own cat. The babies were sort of cute, like tiny Hummels. Rats are infinitely uglier. You can see each claw, the nakedness of the tail. Fur is like a

baby, sweet. Naked is "I'm an animal, not a pleasant one. Thanks for the cheese."

Wishes, dreams, regrets, could-have-beens,
long-losts, *founds*, and so many deaths captured
in these boxes. Death seems to be a major theme:
programs from memorial services, funeral cards
with a photo and a prayer on the back and the mor-
tician's nice way of saying that the big eraser came
and rubbed them out—sunrise on this day, sunset
on that one. When Sam was five, he asked if we'd
die on the same day, and when I said I would die
first because I was much older, he began to weep.
After a minute he said, "If I had known that, I
wouldn't have agreed to be born."

So much of his childhood art is in these boxes—
Maybe he'll have a show someday!—and every
school picture from preschool. Why, there's that
little Christian girl who sank her front teeth into
Sam's forehead. That's what love looks like at three
years old. I wonder how she turned out. Probably
MAGA. There is so much stuff in the attic that we
don't want, never knew we kept, or will never use,
pants that will never fit again, all shoved alongside things that remind us of life's extraordinary
beauty.

There's no coherent filing system in an attic
because it's where you put things that you can't

file, unless you were reduced to labeling your bankers boxes "Who I tried or pretended to be or thought I was" and a personal favorite, "Worst decisions of all." Why haven't I thrown away every last scrap of proof that I stayed with a semi-famous writer for a year who made a hook nose with his finger every time he mentioned his own Jewishness? Whose girlfriend when we met was twenty-five years younger than he? Oh my! Look at all the pretty red flags. A week later his agent told mine he was over the moon and I thought this was good news. An addictive year together led to a spectacularly bad ending. I don't throw out the meager reminders of us—a card, an ugly ring, a Polaroid—because all that pain got me to where I am now. The lasting poison nearly did me in, and from it I wrote the best book of my life.

Susan B. Anthony's grandniece, also named Susan B. Anthony, was a sober journalist and counselor, who wrote, "We remember to remember." We remember in the darkest times that the light has always returned with its poor dangly string. People like to say that time heals all wounds, and I think that is very nice but not entirely true: time does heal most things to some extent, and love gently tends the parts that still hurt.

When I moved my mother into memory care, I

saved her heavy suitcase that contained every bit of correspondence she had ever received from anybody, including every postcard. They were proof that she was loved, or had been, and this brought us both happiness.

What made it impossible for my mom to throw out any of it—and you may well ask, impossible for me to, even after she died? Here were people who made a sweet and polite effort to reach out to her, and so she was not going to just read it and throw it in the trash. Friends took the time to write to her and find a stamp. They thought of Nikki back in Marin and grace moved them to say, "We are here and thinking of you." That is love.

Do I actually plan to leave all *my* stuff for my family to sort through when I am gone? Probably. I did it for my parents; my kid can do it for me. The old ways are the best ways.

The spiders go over it and over it, looking for something I can't see. They scuttle out when you open each box. As a kid my older brother was actively terrified by spiders and spiderwebs, hating that the webs could get all over your face, stick to your lips, your nose and eyes. And there could be spiders hiding motionless in them, hairy little agents of death. Men tend to be so much more afraid of spiders than women. They could squash them, but they are both scuttly and weirdly kind of delicate, and when flattened turn gucky. Women are so much better with guck. Plus, it's not a fair fight. You can't go mano a mano with a spider.

It can be so scary just being here on Earth that we find things to fixate on to make it less galactic: my brother with spiders, me with snakes. Once when we were children my brother dropped a baby garter snake down the front of my sunsuit. Today I have no idea whether I actually took an Advil ten minutes ago or simply meant to, but I absolutely remember that the sunsuit was faded aqua with tiny white flowers and tied at the shoulders.

The little snake got past the elastic waist, and I screamed until my dad fished it out. I can still feel it slithering around on my belly.

I have only a small box capturing my time with Neal so far, mostly pictures of our vacations, wedding, brochures, receipts, trinkets from cathedral gift shops. I saved a photo of a day in Greece when Neal and I had a fight, a big one for us, when he tried to casually correct something I'd said in the book I was writing. I tried to ignore him, but he is a know-it-all and he all but had to pull over on the road to Athens to browbeat me with his superior knowledge. We had several arctic hours in the car and then we arrived at the familiar truth that a

good marriage is one where each person thinks he
or she got the better deal. The photo is of a beach
between two harbors where we'd swum earlier underneath a cerulean sky. We'd made up by dinner.
But I remember. It helps that Neal confessed that
he was wrong, and upon doing so did not die.

Many mementos are from times I do not remember because I was drunk, including one award
I received in a blackout, an unpublishable manu-
script, photos of men I spent my twenties and earliest thirties with when I was so impaired that in
one case I had to all but army crawl across the floor
of my houseboat to get us the platter of cocaine.
The man liked that kind of spunk in a girl. The
tray was an engraved silver platter I had won at
tennis in Canada at sixteen. I liked to keep it around
to remember that I had once moved about like a
dream and had not always been the wired wreck
who brought the platter to the boyfriend like a gei-
sha. I need to remember what I was like before the
miracle.

There are so many photos of happy times, cakes
and balloons, photos of people I have shown up to
celebrate and who celebrated me. I saved the loving and funny birthday cards they gave me, all of
which the silverfish savor. (Who thought up these

teeny armored insects who hide their work until you take out a piece of paper and see that it has become lace, like an Alzheimer's brain, who have slipped away through the wall's invisible cracks?)

When my husband and I moved into this ramshackle ruin of a home, there was only one bedroom. We had to envision and create spaces for my son and grandson until we could convert the barn into a cottage. And we did. A carpenter friend magically jiggled some rooms into being and Neal grew a glorious garden. But there was not much storage.

One day I got it in my head that our builder friend could convert the attic above our bedroom into an elegant storage space for our boxes, with good lighting and a cute rag rug in the middle, a Beatrix Potter reading room. And I could not let this vision go.

Neal's unreasonable position, backed up by the builder, was that creating this in our attic would cost a small fortune, not get us much space, and ruin the looks of the minuscule room where Jax was going to live. Pick, pick, pick. I still wanted it. Neal and our builder pretended they were considering various plans to make this happen. In the meantime, I said my best prayer: Help. Show me the way. And She did. I heard: Let it go, babe: trust Me on this. This time the men are right. I hate when God does not agree with my excellent ideas, but I sighed and unclenched my grip.

Instead we looked up to the hills from whence our help cometh, as promised. And in our case we noted the hillock above the rest of the property on which sat a rotted-out rusty storage shed. Voilà. We looked at each other, smiled, and hired a couple of very nice hungover meth-heads to tear it down and in its place install a big handsome Tuff Shed from Home Depot. It somehow holds all of our stuff—his family's, mine, my new daughters' and sons', and the gear and toys for when Neal's very grand granddaughter visits. It looks over our daily lives and we visit it often, wondering where our snow clothes are amid all those boxes, and then we see the small pretty floral one holding our wedding mementos—the plastic leis, our handwritten vows, my Italian flower barrettes. Meanwhile, there is still nothing in the attic, not one scrap of paper. We go to sleep safely below its emptiness. Neal falls right to sleep, while I read for hours by the light of my tablet. When I finally turn it off, I can feel the empty chamber over me, the shadows and critters and dust, but sometimes I also imagine I can feel the moonlight on my lids through its window. Something inside you knows when you're sleeping that the moon is shining on you and on half the world, and even though it may be very dark in the room, the moon's shy light is present. It silvers the wavering dark, as if the night is an ocean.

NINE

Fog of Love

The night was socked in with fog when we left our home for a red-eye flight to Cuba. We could not see anything on either side of the Golden Gate Bridge, only the lights of the cars ahead of us, adding a sense of intrigue and confusion. Having lived my whole life in the Bay Area, I am friends with fog, with its waves, its tendrils, how it rolls across the hills of the headlands, minute droplets that can somehow carpet the city, the bay, the world, and a sudden illumination when the light sneaks through, then dips back into uncertainty. Fog is a dreamscape of revelation and obscurity, of ruined outdoor parties and blessed relief from the heat. It is mystical and common, sometimes annoying, often gorgeous, then bland, and shifting back and forth, a bit like life.

I had always dreamed of going to Cuba, the strange, tropical destination with its bright music and flavors and sun, but when I finally got there, I dreamed dark.

Havana isn't dark, though, but light-filled and lively, with a surprising amount of silliness for a police state. Absolutely destitute, the people are lovely, affable, peaceful, neither optimistic nor pessimistic but rather resigned. With a mean monthly income of about thirty-five dollars nobody was complaining.

Well, except for me.

The cell service was terrible! Texting was erratic, and even worse, there was almost no Wi-Fi at our rental. You couldn't calm yourself after a day amid extreme privation with a binge at Amazon or eBay. You couldn't find out the latest dirt about the royal family or Marjorie Taylor Greene. And outside the comfort of our private room, there was a dire lack of toilet paper, not to mention toilet seats. I would be a terrible communist: "From each according to his ability, to each according to his needs"? Nah, not me. I'm all about the internet, toilet paper, places to buy lattes and lip gloss. We couldn't stay in any of the fancy hotels because of the US trade embargo rules, but we loved our *casa particular*, Havana Dream, a rental with our own bathroom, a simple breakfast every morning, and the most marvelous young manager named Patricia Jiménez Duany. Patricia, pronounced Pa-tree-see-ah, could, on occasion, scare up some Wi-Fi. I'd race back to the mother ship every afternoon, past crumbling buildings that looked like they'd been bombed, people literally living on air and government rations, to the option of watching three staticky government-owned TV stations. I pined for Wolf Blitzer.

I hadn't been in Cuba twenty-four hours before I awoke from a dream in which one of my best friends, Janine, broke up with me, told me that I was needy, ridiculous, and unlovable, and that everyone thought this. She repeated: *everyone*.

Hmmmph. As if I need someone else to tell me.

I told Neal my dream and he said that everyone worth their salt shares this fear, including anyone I might ever agree to have dinner with. In dreams, scary things get out, and everything shows, everything that has been lurking innocuously behind the fog. "I like fog," I protested. I like frosted windows. I like a lid on things.

"But then that stuff runs you," he pointed out.

Oh yeah, there's that.

After breakfast, we hit the cobblestone streets. The buildings on both sides are so close together that there is a lot of shade. The light sneaks around buildings like a spy, comes down and hits objects that are already illuminated. I texted Janine and told her my dream. "Not breaking up!" she wrote back. "Doomed without you."

In my favorite photo of us, she's looking down pensively as the camera clicks. We are sitting together on her couch. She is listening. I see comfort and receptivity in her face. We often have girl-friendly chatter, but in this photo you see a deep heart connection, an absolutely unprotected person, in tender vulnerability and openness. I see in that photo and in quiet talks an intimate, intuitive love. In the photo, she was the recipient, I was the channel; delivering, receiving. This is the nature of love.

We were staying in Old Havana, a fifteen-minute walk to the Malecón, the seawall across the bay from the fortress built in the 1500s to guard the entrance to the Havana harbor. Some mornings we walked out of the hubbub of the city streets to find fog hovering over the bay, like a gentle drop toward introspection. Everywhere were baroque and neoclassical monuments side by side with pastel houses in ruins, some buildings are as ornate as you'd see in the French Quarter of New Orleans, with balconies and fine wrought-iron gates. Most of the buildings in our neighborhood had multiple molting layers of formerly bright paint, a pentimento of old layers and brushstrokes, so faded it's like a forgotten fresco, the original colors lost to time, both sorry-looking and gorgeous. There were eighteenth-century Spanish buildings, elegant, colonnaded and balconied. Most houses had layers and layers of plaster that had peeled off irregularly, so they looked like archaeological digs that had been recently unearthed.

We walked the narrow streets, cooled by breezes from the bay. Neal and I always talk easily but still, sometimes I need a break. In Cuba, however, there weren't many ways to get one because it's so populated, loud, and intense. One of the few ways was to try to text people. I stopped to text Janine with my sudden idea for a game show called *Why They Hate You*, where a panel of people describe what is so awful about each contestant: Two-faced! Too eager to please or impress! Desperate for things to run smoothly! C'est moi.

There is music on nearly every block, reggaeton, Afro-Cuban *son*, and jazz. Neal can talk music of almost any kind with extreme erudition. I just tune him out. There are also millions of cats, as if when we weren't looking, God released a bulging burlap sack of them. We didn't see a single mouse or rat.

Images of Che and Fidel are ubiquitous, especially Che, yet most of the boys and young men were in T-shirts and tank tops of American sports heroes they love, most frequently Steph Curry and LeBron. When I pointed and called out the Warriors or Giants, I got a smile. Go, Gonzaga. Roll Tide! Thumbs up.

Walking back to Havana Dream, we passed a few policemen, unarmed, bored. Cuba is a very nice police state, as police states go, compared to Israel, say, where thousands of heavily armed young people study you with gimlet eyes, which, whether they need to or not, is a bit stressful. Patricia got me half an hour of Wi-Fi heaven. We'd been afraid of missing any random perp walks and news of the storms back home, which we later learned tore out our manzanita by the roots. The storm had abated. I texted my son and grandson to see how they were faring and if they had electricity, but it wouldn't go through. I wondered if they were even alive.

One morning when we walked to the Malecón,

a heavy fog hung over the harbor. Fog gives you a peaceful, illuminated, rhythmical place to rest your eyes. When it is really thick, it plays peek-a-boo with nature. You don't know what it conceals—the bay, a forest, a town? Trees typically poke their treetops through rather comically—we're trees, this is what we do! Fog makes trees happy because it's like an aerosol watering.

But Havana's fog could not stand up for long to the hot egg-yolk sun.

Neal and I are comfortable chamois shirts with each other now, always interested in what the other thinks about politics, books, God, but the fog of love is gone. In the months after first meeting, we saw each other every single day, mooning idiots until one tragic day when he flew off to his college reunion in Santa Fe. He was to be gone for five days, but on the third day he took a five a.m. flight back from Albuquerque to be with me. The fog of love was a cocktail of barbiturates with a lot of caffeine—heaven to an old addict like me.

Walking endlessly through Havana, we kept finding ourselves at an outside tourist bar at the public square near where we were staying. An excellent band on the terrace played roughly ten hours a day, with a lead guitarist, bass player, horn player, and rotating percussion players and singers. They were absolutely brilliant musicians, world class, free to all.

Everything in Cuba was broken or breaks. Cuba even makes the stuff you brought with you break. The strap of my bag broke on our second day, so I bought a handmade straw backpack, which later that same day popped its button closure. The button had been attached by a wire twist tie that dropped off when I was not paying attention. Someone would inevitably find it and use it to repair a car or close a wound during surgery. Then the straw purse-strings broke. I put some money in it and gave it to the astonished little girl across the street from our place. The next day I bought a pretty cloth backpack that I loved for the three days before the straps ripped out.

The police stop and talk to people, mostly those they just want to move along. But they're not touching people while they're talking to them, not aggressing in any way. They seem like good guys. You see them indicating rather gently to the prostitutes and the homeless that they need to move. There aren't many homeless people because family is so strong. Three generations live in every hovel and they have to take especially tremendous care of each other these precarious days: the economy has taken a beating since COVID choked off the tourist money, and there is so little of everything except potato chips. There is only the good vibe of people who have almost nothing but the beauty of creation and the desire to help each other come through. Also, government-issued buns for breakfast every day, part of the food ration, in tempting shades of taupe.

In a ten-minute walk from our *casa particular*, you could, as Neal had said, encounter eighty percent of everything that is true and beautiful. You could experience joy and sensory pleasures, the colors, the bright classic cars, coffee and peanuts roasting, the music, chatter. And you could feel so sad, deeply moved by the people, their suffering and their loving warmth. The tenderness within families was so dear I had to look away sometimes. I often found Neal looking downward as we walked, deep in thought, which was actually the pose in the photo of his online dating profile that attracted me. When he is listening to me most attentively, he often looks down. It makes it safe for me to talk freely. Sometimes I am looking down, too. Sometimes the only way you can deliver truth to a loved one is to start from deep inside, let it rise up through the chest and out the mouth, and then waft downward to the earth, the rug, a lap.

This is so different, this untangled love. In my childhood, when someone looked down, it often meant they didn't want to look at you. And if *I* was looking down, it might be an opportunity for a sibling to snatch something I was holding onto, like Snoopy grabbing Linus's blanket. I'd complain or cry, a parent would sort things out, and then something sweet and doggy might happen soon after. This is the nature of family love.

Neal does deep research wherever we travel, so he could get us onto public transportation, to good restaurants, to the Museum of the Revolution. Me? Before him, I had always just shown up as Blanche DuBois, so people would help me. His way made it possible for him to lead us through Havana with confidence, and he knew details about where we could get the best fish for dinner, or the hours when the great baroque cathedral is open, or the current exchange rate for Cuban pesos. He admits to being a know-it-all, a fount of information that can drive a girl crazy, yet he is such a decent man. His suitcase was filled with giant bottles of Advil, prenatal vitamins, and baby clothes to give away, all of which are prohibitively expensive here (as he, of course, knew from his research).

One morning he announced that we would be taking public transportation to the beaches. We put on our bathing suits, packed towels, and headed out to the bus stop. Various buses came by, but Neal shook his head, "Nope, not that one . . . nope, not that one." Finally the right one came and we hopped on. It was a thirty-minute drive through Havana, and through a tunnel that eventually led to dunes, scrub, and palm trees. We came to the resort area. There were a number of stops at popular beaches, and so I tapped on the shoulder of the man sitting in front of us and asked, "La playa mas bonita?" Prettiest beach? And he replied, in English, "We get off this one."

Half the bus emptied at Playa Santa María, and we tagged along with the man and his girlfriend, who was exactly half his age and spoke no English: Nelson and Yenny. He would be played in the movies by Hank Azaria at forty, Yenny by Salma Hayek at twenty. We walked through the dunes to the mile-long white diamond sands. The sea was calm, light blue and minty green. We rented a canvas tarp canopy for $6.50, with two rickety chairs thrown in. Nelson urged Neal to speak to him in English so he could practice. There were a thousand people on the beach, all brown and Black except for us, on rented chaise lounges and umbrellas. Nelson invited Neal to swim out to the sandbar.

Yenny and I pantomimed going into the water

together, but as we got up past our waists, she conveyed through shaking her head that this was as far as she could go. I asked, "Sin nadar?" which means "Without swimming?" and sí, sí, she couldn't swim. I said, "Enseño," I teach. And I do. I got her to trust me: she let me hold her by her tummy, and she floated with her head out of the water. "Buena niña!" Good girl. "De nuevo," she demanded, wanting to do it again, and we did, over and over. The guys were talking away on the sandbar, quite far away. I showed her how to kick and held her up while she kicked. I lowered my face into the water and held it there, blowing bubbles, but she made the universal sign of "No way, José." "Vamos," I said. Come on. Yenny took a breath, dipped her head, came out spluttering. She did it again and again, spluttering, laughing. Buena niña! I pantomimed that I was going to hold her up again, and I held her horizontally, and walked her around with her head up until I pushed it gently under. She kicked. I showed her cupped hands, long reaches, scoop scoop, and she swam. We were both screaming and laughing and then I wrapped my aged imperialist running dog arms around her youthful coffee-colored socialist shoulders.

They had brought bag lunches, but Neal and I walked out past the dunes to a man selling

extremely unhygienic chicken and pork sandwiches. There were really no choices. We each got
a small sandwich and ate them standing and then
almost got Yenny and Nelson some beer, but instead we wandered back.

They were still eating when we arrived. "We
almost got you beer," Neal said apologetically, but
Nelson shook his head.

"Not me. I don't drink for twelve years."

I gaped. "Me either," I cried out. "Thirty-seven
years for me, sober!"

"Sí, sobrio. Alcohólicos Anónimos." He palmed
his head. "Bill Wilsonos!" He, like me, had been
fished out of the slough.

I exclaimed, "Ay, caramba," which I thought
meant "Wow" in a happy surprised way, instead of
"Oh no," the actual translation. At any rate, we
gripped each other, brother and sister under the
hot Cuban sun.

Neal and I took the bus back to town, and he
walked me toward our room for my afternoon nap.
I loved Havana, but a few times I felt like I was
beyond done and had to leave right that minute.
However Neal loved it so much and I love him and
that gave me the willingness to stay friendly far
outside my comfort zones. He makes all of my life
so much easier, even bearable. On *Why They Hate*

You the panel would say, "She is such a scaredy-cat." I am often afraid and Neal makes me feel both safe and braver. That, too, is the nature of love.

The single most amazing sight was that almost no one, anywhere, was holding a phone to his or her ear, or thumb typing. Tourists can get some Wi-Fi at their hotels, but Cubans have restricted access to government-sanctioned sites. They can't check in ten times an hour to find out about celebrity scandals or political intrigue. What a nightmare. In spite of or because of this, the vibe is peaceful, whereas in America, people deprived of their phones would look like it was the zombie apocalypse.

After our swim and all that sun, I slept for nearly two hours while Neal walked around, and at some point I dreamed a terrifying dream.

I was walking in the fog, afraid. The fog is concealing the house where my father lives with his last girlfriend, whom we'll call Bev. Bev and my brothers and I were—let's say—not made for each other. It was a miserable situation for her—she and my dad started dating, and four months later he had brain cancer. He moved in with her and she took care of him for almost two years, until one day she asked him to leave, when he was at the mental level of a five-year-old, barely mobile, showed him to the road outside their house and called me to come get him. She had reached her limits. This I understood but did not forgive. He was in his bathrobe.

My nineteen-year-old brother and I took care of Dad the last five months of his life in our one-room family cabin. Bev was there every day helping, and we did the best we could. We were loving and polite with each other. It was profound and beautiful, and it sucked. There was subterfuge that I won't go into here. And after he died, she spirited away the one thing he left behind, besides us, which was a magnificent jazz record collection.

I won't take her inventory here except to say that if Bev had been a contestant on *Why They Hate You*, the panel would have focused on how she viewed her frequently expressed opinions on all of life as revealed truth. We almost never saw her or spoke again after Dad died.

In the dream, Dad appeared through the fog and said that Bev didn't want me to see him for a while because I always made everything worse. Then Bev stepped forth holding a gun and stood beside him. It turned out I had a gun, too. I've never even touched one in real life. I'm pretty sure that if I so much as held one I would end up shooting off my foot, but the dream involved us chasing each other down. Shots were fired. I was prepared to kill her. But then she sat down in a corner, heaving for breath.

I didn't quite know what to do, which is when historically I have experienced the movement of grace in my life. She sat with her knees pulled to her chest. She looked defeated, and she looked at me adoringly. I thought about shooting her. Instead, I slowly, slowly bent down to my knees and cradled her. I said, "I love you. My family can never thank you enough." I stroked her head like a mother or a worried young daughter.

I woke up on my bed in the hot room in Havana in shock. Bev? *Really?* But wait. If you believe Carl Jung, everyone in a dream is us. So this dream about a bossy, greedy person who took the only thing of value my father owned, his records, this prideful woman who thought she was always right and always knew the exact next thing to do was me: darling evolved me. I was Bev and I was the armed and furious Annie who stamped her foot and said "He's mine," and—the universal illusion—"I'm doing the right thing."

The dream was saying to me, "Here's the letter; read it." The letter was leftover pain and anger, hidden way deep inside so I couldn't hear it banging along behind me, like tin cans tied to a wedding car. I couldn't get the letter till my defenses were down. Bev had loved my father and he had loved her; they must have cried together so often. I realized, stupidly, that she had loved me, too. I hadn't really noticed it in the fog of brain cancer, our anger, the daily grief and confusion toward the end. She had fed me, sometimes enjoyed me, put up with my drunkenness and jealousy. The letter was love. Love wears all these clothes, and it's hard to see through all those jackets because love is territorial, love is anxious, and burdened. Rarely can we get a gust of pure love, but I got one in Cuba from the single last place I ever expected to find it.

(A year after my father died, Bev married the medical director of Hospice, who had been at the cabin frequently those last five months when Bev was there, who signed my father's death certificate, and with whom she ended up having a long and apparently happy marriage. God must have been very pleased with God's self.)

Rattled and sad, I texted Neal to come get me for dinner. He got the text and hurried back. I told him about my dream as we walked along toward the Plaza in the heat. He listened intently, looking down, nodding at each detail. I told him I was getting homesick and wanted to go home, to the dogs and the fog, to my friends, church, couch, and hiking trails. We stopped now and then to listen to the music coming out of bars. Neal's god expresses itself through music. Afro-Cuban songs were being played all day and night wherever we went, played seriously by jazz musicians who were improvising, who were brilliant at their instruments and at ease with the genre. You could see how well they were listening to each other, like the best jazz musicians, where you see suddenly that somebody is completely changing the tone and the rhythm, and the other musicians are looking at each other, going, "Huh, this is interesting." And they go somewhere magical, somewhere we can't see.

TEN

General Instructions

I drove to church on Palm Sunday, six days after the latest school shooting. The sky was notable for being blue with fluffy white clouds after two solid weeks of torrential rains. Three more little kids had been shot in Nashville, and three aides; I'd heard a commentator say that the measure of a nation is how many small coffins it allows. I had my Sunday school lesson planned around Jesus riding into town on a young donkey, running the gauntlet of fickle crowds, but as I drove along I realized I couldn't use it. You can't put a nice bow on nightmares. The temptation is to say, as cute little Christians sometimes do, "Oh, it will all make sense someday," but if it minimizes the crucifixion, it's bullshit. What could I do or say today? What can we ever do or say? Thoughts and prayers?

Some friends are moving to Canada next month because they cannot bear what this nation has become, especially MAGA and the school shootings. They seek freedom from their kid being shot at school. That seems a pretty good reason to move. Canada apparently lacks enthusiasm for small coffins: most assault weapons are banned. Those big babies.

I've been teaching the story of Easter since I started a Sunday school at our tiny church in 1994, when my son was a squirmy, bored five-year-old and life made a lot more sense. I came to know firsthand the nightmare many of my students had at home, on the blacktop, in their souls. All we teachers have to offer is our love, listening ears, faith stories, art supplies, and healthy snacks. I'd brought a box of Snyder's pretzels that day.

I told the friends who are moving that they'll come crawling back, that you can't find decent American snacks in Canada—no Cheez-Its, no iconic chocolate miniatures wrapped in festive Easter foil, no Snyder's pretzels. We always have pretzels at Lent. Historians think pretzels were created around the year 600 by monks in a

monastery during Lent, the forty days before Easter, where they would take leftover scraps of dough
from their baking and form them into strips to rep-
resent a child's arms folded in that era's way of
prayer, hands on opposite shoulders.

My newest crop of Sunday school kids includes
four siblings caught in the middle of a catastrophic
divorce. The little one, a tiny nine-year-old girl,
sometimes comes to church in tears. (There is a second nine-year-old from another family who is almost as big as I am, which must be hard.) Two others
are teenagers, and all four of them are brown. Vile
racist things happen to them at school. None of
them had ever gone to church until their parents
showed up at the door, so we teach God 101: God is
love, love is God, they are adored and perfect as is.

All four were there on Palm Sunday, and I no
longer had a plan except to talk with them about
the shooting in Nashville, let them share their feelings, and listen. I actually believed—I had to
believe—that something good would come of this,
but I didn't know yet what that would be, as God
hadn't sent me the email. So I'd be winging it.

We stayed in the big church for the first twenty
minutes of songs and recitations and then were
excused to our small, fabulous classroom, which
has an oval table with chairs. We let the bigger

nine-year-old light the candle in the middle of the table: the light of God, eternal and indwelling. Let there be light, and let it begin with me. (Years ago, one of our teenage girls managed to catch her hair on fire while leaning across the table to flirt with a boy. I think this says it all.) We prayed and passed the high-five peace of God we have adopted since COVID. Because we would be rejoining the grownups for our monthly Communion in about forty-five minutes, I reminded them of the sacrament, grape juice and a bit of sourdough bread—the bread of heaven, as any foodie will confirm.

They are so lovely and innocent, and they wake me up, which is good because I find myself tired much of the time. And they make me laugh. We were recently reviewing some of the things we know about God—love, creator, healer, friend—and one kid announced, blasé, knowingly, "God is basically like a vet." This is exactly right: the love, the enjoyment, the profound care, and sometimes needing to cause pain in order to do the healing.

There should be one rule we all agree to: that you can't shoot children.

I asked them on Palm Sunday if they'd heard about Nashville.

They had. They knew a lot about it. Both nine-year-olds knew that the three dead children had also been nine. My heart sank.

"Did your parents and teachers talk to you about how you feel?"

"Not really," said the eldest, the fourteen-year-old boy. "They just told us it had happened and we saw it on the news. We had a shooter drill at school. My mother cried a lot."

All the other kids nodded. I was about to ask how it left them feeling, but instead I closed my eyes for a moment. I heard, loud and clear, that these kids had had enough for one week. So I moved on to Plan B, which had actually been Plan A, the talk I'd prepared for Palm Sunday and Holy Week. But first I told them almost everything I know about life: that it is a precious gift, and hard; that it is full of pleasures, messes, delights, loss, suffering, love. I also shoehorned in a suggestion that they pour themselves into reading, that this would give them better lives. All good books are books of ourselves. "Promise me you'll all read a lot," I said, and they nodded, and two said at the same time, "I already do."

So, Easter: Jesus weeps as He approaches Jerusalem for all the suffering that awaits its people after the fall of the temple, and for all the suffering of humanity, the violence, ignorance, and evil we see around us. (I did not name names.) Christ suffers, the innocent suffer, it's agony. It's the ongoing tragedy of humans. But Jesus has got the goods, the good news of reckless love. Kids always love the part where Jesus sends a disciple across the street to borrow a donkey to ride into Jerusalem for the feast of Passover. A donkey symbolizes peace, rather than a horse, which announces war, but what the kids and I like is that the owner of the donkey lets the disciple take it instead of shooting him.

The crowds were going wild with welcome.

"You kids know that within a few days, this same crowd will call for His death, out of fear of crossing the men in power? Do you know the word *fickle*? It means when people suddenly change their loyalties. Maybe someone you thought was a good friend cut you off?" But then I heard myself, a jukebox of misery stories. What was I going to tell them next, that their pets will all eventually die? "Yes, children, even little Abby."

But I had to tell them one thing that I wish someone had told me.

"There's an answer for when bad things happen to you or people scare you. Does anyone know what that is?"

They looked around, as if on a panel. "Run,

hide, fight," the teenage boy said. He is right and I cannot stand it.

"Stop, drop, and roll?" the older girl volunteered.

"Yes, in case of fire. Very good."

"Run, hide, stomp, roll," singsonged the bigger nine-year-old.

"Call your mother," the smallest girl said in a tiny quavering voice.

"Yes! Or you tell a teacher, an auntie, or us. Any safe adult. You tell, okay? Secret of life! Read a lot of books and don't keep bad secrets."

They have been taught, as most of us have, to keep bad family stuff secret—but I noticed I was doing it again, making them talk about scary things. I was like some mad bummer lady: Let's talk about acne next, kids.

"Time for a snack," I announced, to stop myself. They looked around: it was early for snacks. I got out the box of Snyder's pretzels—yay, America!—but I was suddenly in sync with the Spirit and I knew what these children needed: sugar! Our church is in a gravely impoverished town amid the obscene wealth of Marin County. We trooped over to the fellowship hall where some of our church members were sorting and packing up masses of donated food to distribute the next day in our food pantry. They gave us festive Easter cupcakes. Jesus would be fine with a cupcake communion. He knew no boundaries when it came to loving children. He was kind of a sap that way.

Back in our room we got out the art supplies to make cards for four lucky kids in Nashville. I could mail them to a friend there to distribute. "It may not seem like much to you," I said, "but because love is God, acts of kindness, compassion, or gen- erosity can be seen as God's grace. Forgiveness is God's love on steroids. Now get to work."

My staunchly atheist father taught English and creative writing to the prisoners at San Quentin in the '50s and '60s, and his humanity was a grace. He knew the prisoners were not free in this world, so he taught them another kind of freedom.

Maybe humanity is another synonym for God.

While they worked on their cards, I told the kids the story of the sparrow and the horse, which I have written about before but which bears repeat- ing. A war horse comes upon a sparrow lying on its back in the street with its feet straight up in the air. "What on earth are you doing?" the horse sneers.

"I'm trying to help hold back the darkness," the sparrow replies.

"That's absurd," the horse says. "You barely weigh an ounce."

"One does what one can," says the sparrow.

The nine-year-olds both looked puzzled. "Is that a true story?" one asked.

I watched them draw, their faces inward and dreamy, their mouths on the edges of smiles— trees, hearts, dogs, and, improbably, a beaver. This will save them, art and imagination, the power of imaginative joy. It tells us we will not plummet to the ground. We will be caught.

Over the last thirty years, while most of my Sunday school kids have done fine with the usual allotment of struggle, loss, disheartening jobs, and missed opportunities—i.e., real life—several of my cherished kids have died. One of brain cancer. One by hanging because she felt she could not come out as gay. And one was shot under the bridge where he was living in a homeless encampment. My kids have been cutters, addicts, and anorexics, and that was before things here got really bad: new scientific reports now say Earth will likely cross the threshold beyond which it can't avoid catastrophic climate change within the next ten years unless we rapidly stop burning fossil fuels. Raise your hand if you think we will. Recent parents have come to me near tears and asked how they can help their kids with this. I tell them that they need to be in prayer about this with their kids, but also that we are good at discovering impossible things, like the God particle and the Hubble Telescope, the human genome and proton radiation. So help them focus on miracles and how each child can help: Be kind, do good. Pick up litter in the neighborhood. Walk more, plant seedlings. Read inspiring biographies with them. Help them find ways to serve the poor. Laugh a lot, read, and make art. That's all I've got.

The kids were so focused, sorting through a box of colored pencils and markers for the exact color they needed. A skirmish broke out when the teenage girl took an orange marker called "marigold" that her older brother wanted. I glared at the boy with what I hoped conveyed biblical dismay.

I talked to them about the Last Supper while they drew, in preparation for Communion.

"Now, I am going to tell you the craziest thing in the Bible," I announced. After the Passover meal of bread and wine, Jesus washed His disciples' feet. He wanted them to know that this was their calling— not to gain power and prestige but to serve others; not to get but to give; to share; to be humble. I told them about the man who told me he'd come into AA as a hotshot but worked his way up to servant. "I know that doesn't make sense," I said, "but serving others is where we often find happiness. And here is the crazy thing I mentioned: Jesus even washed Judas's feet. He knows Judas is about to betray Him to the Roman authorities, which will lead to the crucifixion on Good Friday, and He washes his feet anyway. John doesn't say this in his gospel, but if we count noses in his telling, we know Judas is there in the upper room where Jesus washed *all* the disciples' feet. And this is the Easter message: that you are loved no matter who you think you are, because God can only love. Jesus looked at Judas and saw a dozen forms of suffering—the secrets, the lies, the isolation, the shame—and He loved him. God can't not love. God is baffled by what *isn't* love. God loves, period."

Evil, sickness, and death definitely complicate the picture, but I didn't say this out loud as I was trying to stifle mad bummer lady vibes.

"Why is it called Good Friday if Jesus dies?" The older kids are always my undoing. They ask why little kids get cancer, and why God doesn't stop global warming, and I want to say, "Go figure, right?" But I can tell them that God helps nurses and us care for sick kids. And God gave us Earth to care for, but we got greedy and power mad and we wrecked it. God doesn't cause cancer. Nature does what it does, and God is in the healers among us.

God set creation in motion and will partner with us every step of the way, eliciting a helpful spark within us, the bright, sharp, shining spark we read about in the Hebrew Bible. Be the spark. God gives us hope in science, a calling to help, and this amazing new generation of thinkers and activists. I always add that if I were in charge of things, I would hand God a magic wand, but I guess the magic wand turns out to be worried old us.

How could I explain why the darkest, bleakest day ever is called Good? It was almost time to start cleaning up and I was tired and my first thought was to punt. But I sighed and began.

"We call it Good Friday because it leads to the resurrection, for Him, and for us. The world is dark, sometimes so cruel that it will take your breath away, so Jesus dies to help us change that suffering into meaning, renewal, transformation, eternal life. He dies on Good Friday, and then the women wait in grief at the cross, and on Saturday they wait at the empty tomb for a while. Saturday is dark. There is no sun. But what follows on Sunday morning is Easter. And there is new life. The bulbs bloom. This is our version."

The kids looked at me like, *Wait, what are you saying, old lady? The bulbs bloom. That's it?*

Yeah, pretty much. That and all the love biz.

I sent out a spy to see how much longer the service might last. "Paperwhites are pretty beautiful," I continued, "and daffodils." They were too polite to roll their eyes where I could see them. "Be amazed," I said. "That's Easter. Be amazed and be comforted. As my friend Barbara wrote, 'We are Easter people living in a Good Friday world. It gets colder and darker, and then the morning comes.'"

The spy returned and reported that Pastor Floyd was still preaching. It meant we had a little while longer until we were summoned for Communion.

I had an idea. "You know how I said that along with sad things, life is full of delights? Let's go find some. Let's take a ten-minute walk."

It was a beautiful day. Our church garden was bursting with flowers and trees in blossom, birds everywhere, mourning doves, chickadees. "Listen," I said, stopping to point at a plum tree. "She'll sing, chick-a-dee-dee-dee," and we listened till she came through. Wildflowers poked through the grass, California poppies, of course, and sour grass. Above were cotton-ball clouds, woolly puffs of breath. As all children have done since we first appeared on this planet, they saw shapes in the clouds, a shark, a buffalo, and a blimp.

"What does it look like to you?" I asked my quiet teenage girl.

We all stared upward as one. After a moment, she said, "Sheepy."

The waterfalls would be rushing all over the county, but we couldn't see or hear any from these flatlands. I commanded them to get their parents to help them find one after church. "When you come upon one, be very quiet, and listen to the roaring crashing sound." Their parents either will or they won't, but I definitely will. I love velocity and plummet when I'm not in it; it's a big inspiring whoosh. I pointed out the golden patches that dotted the deep intense green of a local hill, where grass must have died or was late responding to the rain.

"I could lie down on one of those golden blankets right now," I said. The two oldest kids exchange a look, like *Uh, okay, dying teacher lady, whatev.*

We walked a bit farther. These kids have hard lives and I would like for things to make sense for them. But there can be meaning without things making sense if we are kind and giving. Humane is what makes sense when all else fails. The nine-year-old girls held hands. We scuffled along and then I pointed to the blue above us and shook my head with wonder. "Did you *ever* think we'd have a warm, dry day again?" They squinted up to where birds flew, clouds drifted, the sun shone, and even the moon could be seen. The sky takes you out into the cosmos, reminding you that you are very tiny but can experience celestial wonders and oceans of love here, even just slogging along together beneath a perfectly ordinary sky.

Glimmers

"Man is born broken. He lives by mending.
The grace of God is glue."

—Eugene O'Neill

I have quoted my own version of a William Blake line for so long now that I like to think it's mine: We are here to learn to endure the beams of love. I have lived by these words for nearly fifty years, ever since I first read the quote. It is the sentence I want my family to remember when I am gone. (Also, I hope they forget that someone else said it and that I get the credit.)

This is a radical idea, absolutely contrary to everything I was raised to believe. I was taught to strive, to feel ashamed, to keep the family secrets, to believe I was better than, yet always in danger of lagging behind. I was taught to judge and surpass and above all to showcase a shiny surface of confidence, individualism, and self-sufficiency. We were not a playful family; we were amused. I was taught to observe other people's mediocrity and general ruin, and to make quiet and arch comments about it. What Blake is saying is that none of those things are who I am or why I am here. But without them, who on earth am I? Still a student? Aging, set in her ways—*moi?*

And to bear the beams of love: What a nightmare. No thanks. The cold vibrating spaces inside us protect us and keep us on our toes. Love breaks your heart and love makes you soft. It gets in past your Brooks Brothers armor and makes your skin as permeable as the little green tree frog my friend Caroline found in her shower. If you practice enduring people's bewildering love for you, it will change you molecularly: it loosens you, gooses you, warms you. Bearing the beams of love can dislodge ancient sachets of joy, pain, shame, and pride trapped inside you, and make you smell strange and funny, like soup.

So maybe don't.

You are not stupid. Love can leave bruises on the heart, an oceanic ache. When you give someone your best love, you too are filled with warmth. The world can be so lame, disappointing, and even mean, like an alcoholic father towering over us. But we can't give up on love batting last or we are truly doomed. As Carl Sagan said, "For small creatures such as we, the vastness is bearable only through love."

I consulted my six-year-old colleague to see if he could amplify his earlier statement that love is, well, you know, this stuff.

"Tell me more, if you can," I said. "What is love?"

He thought this over a moment. "It's like, you know—*duh*."

That is all we need to know, not the Greek delineations from Eros, passionate love, to *agape*, selfless divine love; or my own addition, *mascotas*, the love of our animals. It's this feeling, this energy exchange of affection, compassion, kindness, warmth, hope. Duh.

We are here to learn to endure the beams of love. "We" means humankind. Well, there's the rub. That's the fly in the ointment. The best of us can be raging narcissists, annoying, petty, misguided, and so self-destructive. What a sorry, scary bunch we can be. My friend Father Terry Richie once said you have to learn not to have a broken heart after learning there are people all over this country who would volunteer to work for free in a death camp.

And yet, *we.* Wow. You'll be at some horrible party you couldn't get out of and everybody's making small talk, and your entire being seizes up, but then suddenly you glimpse your person across the room, your partner or friend, your dad, a co-conspirator. There is a blip of eye contact and it is a beautiful cellular moment of connection. That can happen on a communal level sometimes, as when sober alcoholics find some other sober people in their meeting rooms, even if they don't understand the language being spoken. Or two families with troubled teens who make eye contact at a gathering of ebullient, successful kids, and exchange expressions of sympathy, of "make this stop." Those are *we* moments we can't even name because they're so holy.

People say pain shared is pain divided. In shared pain, the true self shows: fragile, vulnerable, interdependent and needy. And there's something strong and wonderful about that.

Love and Blake say, "We are here." And here can be so tough and fraught, in our families, bedrooms, cities, and hearts, even without the seas and fascism rising. Human is hard. The temptation is to burnish the appearance of being in full command, to impress, entertain, or dominate. But part of the sorrow is the poignancy of how quickly it all passes, and you can't scam your way out of that. This life is a limited time offer. You are here on the space-time continuum, vulnerable to a dozen kinds of fear, from losing your beloved or your mind to the acronym for Frantic Effort to Appear Relevant. We are here, too, however. We are together. You need us, and we need you. It's a system.

I sometimes despair for my son and grandchild because these are going to be the good old days for them. No one can say what awaits them when I am gone, but it will by all accounts be tough and hot. They will be here when the news breaks that the last cube of sea ice has melted, so for now I try to model crazy redeeming love: my face got imprinted with the chain-link fence while watching my Little League grandson pitch for the first time. I bring home stragglers for our holiday meals and they become family, old-timers when the next feast rolls round. I take care of people who are dying and I perform wedding ceremonies. I get my son and grandson out to our yard for every full moon, the yearly explosion of camellias on the bush outside the plate glass window, the melancholy penny whistle of the golden-crowned sparrow when she

swings by in the fall. I make them come watch
the neighbor's baby grandson practicing his first
drunken steps on the sidewalk. I try to show them
the endless ways to a lasting relationship with love.
Story, song, nature, silence, eating together, helping others out, letting others help me. Life 101. I
have to believe that that should do it.

All of us walk through the doors of a very few
houses that are not our own, and they feel like
home. Everything is where it was—the loving,
poorly behaved dog; the spouse reading a magazine on the couch; the guitar on its stand, just so.
Everything outside the door is changing but not
inside, this is still here, the old tune, just like we
remembered it. Phew. Inside the door, time settles
into its slot just right, with nowhere to race off to,
and certain chords are played for the umpteenth
time, a few notes that plunge us into memories and
laughter, a resonance, the music going from major
to minor and back, encompassing the shadow as
well as the light. This old love is like homemade
bread.

Love is food and medicine. Miracle Max said in
The Princess Bride, "True love is the best thing in
the world, except for cough drops." Love is the few
places where you feel safe, the few faces imprinted
on your soul.

Somehow

The phrase "to learn" now fills me with dread as it implies remembering things. I am trying to learn Spanish and yet when I was trying to teach the young woman Yenny in Cuba to swim, I could not remember for the longest time that *nadar* meant "to swim," although I had learned it *literally* two days before. Having somehow pulled it out of the ether in time to teach her, I couldn't remember it the very next day when I went to write about it. When I RSVP to an invitation or doctor's appointment, I sometimes can't remember half an hour later if I did, or just imagined having done so. But Picasso said, "I am always doing that which I cannot do, in order that I may learn how to do it." I am slowly learning to do the hardest work of all, to love and forgive myself, weirdness and wounded ego and all, and learn the gentle practices—touch, tea, a pretty shirt—that elicit this. Then I forget them.

This is who all of us are, in some degree or another, even my grandson. Jax is gorgeous, like some type of deity. His portrait should be on a temple banner riding a tiger or something, but he will also have the bouts of bad self-esteem that all good people have. What will help are sustaining realms where he is loved and gets to be loving. Maybe he will have a church like I do, the music gloriously imperfect and fervent, a warmth that pours out and surrounds us palpably in this cold world, a bare-bones quality with room for undistracted spirit to expand. Or maybe he'll have a lifelong garage band with friends; it's the same thing. He will live beneath many attics over the years filled with boxes of memorabilia, and he will have the offspring of the rats I have upstairs right now, making merry on this sinking ship, whipping those naked tails about. But inside those boxes will be reminders of times when love could be captured in a photo or card. Fill those boxes, kid. Look through them when you have lost hope. Lift out what you find—saved letters, souvenirs, cards, photos. Love is why we have hope.

"To endure" is not in Blake's original line. He actually wrote "to bear." But "endure" really says it. God, what we have endured, what we have borne, in every life, in our workplaces, families, various disconcerting administrations, family court. Every human has something to cry about, Jeanne Moreau once proclaimed in a great comic performance. When pressed for why this is so, she said, "The winds of solitude roaring at the edge of infinity." I love this. Love is a windbreaker, fashioned of people who sat and listened and got us tea, who did not run for their cute little lives when ours got dark.

Who tucked us in. Who got us to our feet and back outside, reminding us to lift our eyes to the hills.

Our modest mountain was nearly black with dark fog when I got up the other day in full doom mode. Then the sun muscled its way through until the very last of the fog draped itself around the mountain's shoulders in rosy pink, like a feather boa. Love has always (eventually) lifted me out of the swamp of hardship. I heard someone once say that grief is love that is homeless, but in long stretches of grief, people have brought me their bravest selves, willing to help bear my sadness and feel like shit with me. That is true love. When they had to leave, I was a little less clenched; love as massage.

The people we've endured, God almighty! Don't even get me started. Our difficult parents in old age (with their coupons!), the scary teenagers, the niece—a three-year-old, formerly an angel, who galloped through the house like Edith Bunker, bossing everyone around in a loud, nasty way. We dreaded her. She grew into a lost and difficult teenager, but the family managed to love her in spite of it all, and she now teaches ballroom dancing at a local convalescent home.

Some of our kids didn't make it. But then, impossibly, their parents endured, more or less. Month after month, they sat before unchanging windows of gray, crying and crying. Their picture window was spattered by a pointillism of pain, a steady percussive drone, and it never ceased until one day it was a slightly lighter gray fog. A wind tossed the palm trees' branches below, and they were finally curious about them again because a little sun had somehow broken through. Curiosity leads to wonder and wonder is a cousin to love. Wonder is why we are here.

And ah, the beams of love. They're everywhere, particles in everything, like when a packet of jam leaks in a spaceship and infinitesimal specks end up in every molecule. You're feeling doomed—on your own behalf, or your child's or nephew's, or Ukraine's or Malawi's. Then someone or something emerges, stage left—a parent, a friend, an election, a dog, a train ticket, a relative—and there is a new feeling in your heart. Your soul does not want to jinx this, but secretly it cannot help doing a double take with relief or quiet joy. There is still a dark place just out of sight, but also there's a sneaky, mystical, jagged slash of light, a reflection that says, "This is the dark, but we have some light, as well." You hadn't known that. It had not seemed possible, not in the natural world. To experience feelings not of this world is to experience soul. To know the soul is to know love.

I'll tell you what Blake actually wrote more than two hundred years ago: "And we are put on earth a little space, that we may learn to bear the beams of love." If the younger ones in our lives can remember only this one idea, that they are here, briefly, a little space to love and to have been loved, then they will have all they need, because love is all they need, rain or shine—love, cough drops, and one another. Good old love, elusive and steadfast, fragile and unbreakable, and *always* there for the asking; always, somehow.

Acknowledgments

I am grateful beyond words to my editor and dear friend, Jake Morrissey, and my dearest agent, Sarah Chalfant. Thank you, Geoff Kloske, Ashley Garland, Karen Wise, Anna Jardine, and everyone at Riverhead Books.

My closest friends help me with my work every step of the way—Doug Foster, Janine Reid, Neshama Franklin, my two Jesuit sidekicks Fathers Tom Weston and Jim Harbaugh, and Mark Yaconelli. Hugest love and thanks. Doomed without you. Seriously.

Nadia Bolz-Weber and my brilliant cousin Bob Morgen have stepped in many times with charming wisdom.

My bridesmaids, aka the Grandmothers, keep